SPIRITUAL RENEWAL

ANDREW MURRAY

SPIRITUAL RENEWAL

90 DEVOTIONS FOR A
DEEPER FELLOWSHIP WITH GOD

WHITAKER
HOUSE

SPIRITUAL RENEWAL
90 Devotions for a Deeper Fellowship with God

ISBN: 978-1-64123-723-9
eBook ISBN: 978-1-64123-724-6

Printed in the United States of America
© 2021 by Whitaker House

Whitaker House
1030 Hunt Valley Circle
New Kensington, PA 15068
www.whitakerhouse.com

Library of Congress Control Number: 2021945790

CONTENTS

SECTION TWO: THE SECRET OF THE CROSS

SECTION THREE: THE SECRET OF THE ABIDING PRESENCE

THE SECRET
OF THE FAITH LIFE

The great majority of Christians are content with the initial faith that gives the pardon of sin and the hope of eternal life. But they have little idea of the wonderful promises of God given to a full and strong faith—promises that He will cleanse the heart, so that they will love the Lord with all their hearts and all their souls (see Matthew 22:37); promises that He will write the law in their hearts by His Spirit (see Jeremiah 31:33), so that His children can boldly say, *"I delight to do thy will, O my God"* (Psalm 40:8); promises that He will instill fear of Him in their hearts, so that they will never depart from Him (see Jeremiah 32:40); and promises that He will perfect them *"in every good work"* (Hebrews 13:21) to do His will.

Such promises are regarded by most as being altogether beyond the sphere of practical religion; they may be beautiful ideals, but it is simply an impossibility to experience them. Those who look on God's promises in this way have never come to know the almighty power with which God is willing to work in their lives. They have never known how completely the Holy Spirit can take possession of a person who is utterly given up to God, how literally Jesus Christ can dwell and live His life in the heart that is fully surrendered to Him.

As I think of such promises, I feel that I have inadequately shown that in every approach to God, we ought to come with an ever larger faith to worship this great and holy Being, who is able to work in us beyond what we can ask or think. (See Ephesians 3:20.) Some who have read this far may feel that this book is not for them; they know they are Christians, but they do not have time for what so evidently appears beyond their reach. They do not have the time to listen as

9

we call them to come and think of an almighty God and what He is able to do in fulfillment of His Word. They do not have the time or courage to enter into a school for the deeper life; they trust in Christ and are willing to do their utmost to serve Him, even though it is on a lower level.

But there are others, I am sure, whose hearts are yearning for something better than what they have known. They earnestly desire to know Jesus Christ, their loving Redeemer, in the power of the Holy Spirit that He has promised—to serve Him with the love that keeps His commandments and always abides in His love. They are eager to know the secret cause of their feebleness, their unbelief, their inability to influence others around them, or their failure in every attempt to live the prayer life in the joy of daily personal fellowship with Christ Jesus.

It is to such individuals that this section has been written, with the one desire of pointing out the path that leads to the full knowledge of and love for God. The main ideas presented here are very simple and yet very profound. Almighty God, for whom nothing is too difficult, offers to work in them with His omnipotent power every day what they need for the kind of life He wants them to live.

This almighty and most loving God justly claims that they must surrender their entire beings—their lives, their time, and their strength—every day to His keeping and to the fulfillment of His commands. God is to be waited on every day with a childlike confidence that He will reveal Himself as God to work out His will in them. Everything depends on giving the almighty God His place, on yielding our entire lives to His service and His working in us; then we will have the conscious assurance that His mighty power will work in us what we consider impossible.

May every reader be brought under the deep conviction of how such an almighty God, with His wonderful promises, deserves to be met with a strong, wholehearted faith in every approach to Him. He is worthy of it, and nothing less will suffice for our daily lives than a faith that takes possession of and masters our entire selves and always keeps us waiting on God, entirely at His disposal.

The whole God offers Himself to us. Does this blessed and most glorious God not have the right to demand that the whole man, through every moment of his life, be yielded up to Him? Is it not an absolute necessity in the very nature of things?

In this study of what God wants His people to be and what He undertakes to make them, let us beware of only thinking of ourselves. Let each discovery of God's wonderful grace lead us to think of the church of Christ around us, and how little God's children realize what their wonderful privileges in Christ are. As an increasing number of those who are seeking to fully follow the Lord take up the burden of their fellowmen and plead with God for them, we can expect God to visit His people with the revival of the abundant life in Christ, which will make them the power that they are meant to be in the world.

As God's intercessors, we should night and day before Him bear the burden of the low state of the church, the great majority of believers, and even many in the ministry. As we forget ourselves and plead for what appears impossible, we will enter more deeply into the fellowship of Christ and His sufferings, as well as that of Christ and His victory. Such prayers will indeed be fruitful for our own souls and for the world around us.

A PRAYER

Ever blessed God and Father, how can we praise You for the wonderful salvation that You have prepared for us in Christ Jesus? We humbly confess that we have so little understood it, believed it, yielded ourselves to its power, and shown forth its beauty to the world around us.

We fervently pray for all saints, that You would give them a vision of the abundant life that is in Christ Jesus. May this stir their hearts to a deep, unquenchable desire to know fully what Christ is meant to be to them. May they feel deeply

11

that all the powerlessness of Your church to bless the world is the result of not giving Christ and His Holy Spirit the place in their hearts that You desire to have.

Above all, grant such an insight into the need, power, and blessedness of a simple wholehearted faith in Jesus Christ, and such an unreserved surrender to His mastery, that their hearts may be prepared to receive Him in all the fullness of His love and of His abiding presence.

Father, we ask You to hear us in the name of Jesus. Give to each reader such a vision of Your power to fulfill in us every promise, and such a humble childlike trust in Your faithfulness, as will be to Your glory. May all the glory be Yours forever. Amen.

THE IMAGE OF GOD

And God said,
Let us make man in our image, after our likeness.
—Genesis 1:26

Here we have the first thought of man in the mind of God; here man's origin and his destiny are shown to be entirely divine. God undertook the stupendous work of making a creature, who is not God, to be a perfect likeness of Him in His divine glory. Man was to live in entire dependence on God and to receive directly and unceasingly from Him the inflow of all that was holy and blessed in the Divine Being. God's glory, His holiness, and His love were to dwell in man and shine through him.

When sin had done its terrible work and had spoiled the image of God, the promise was given in Paradise of the woman's seed, in whom the divine purpose would be fulfilled: God's Son, *"the brightness of his glory, and the express image of his person"* (Hebrews 1:3), was to become a son of mankind. In Christ, God's plan would be carried out, His image revealed in human form. The New Testament speaks of those who are *"predestinate to be conformed to the image of his Son"* (Romans 8:29) and of *"the new man, which is renewed in knowledge after the image of him that created him"* (Colossians 3:10). We are given the promise: *"We know that, when he shall appear, we shall be like him; for we shall see him as he is"* (1 John 3:2).

Between God's eternal purpose for man and its eternal realization, we have a wonderful promise in regard to life here on earth: *"We all...beholding...the glory of the Lord, are changed into the same image from glory to glory, even as by the Spirit of the Lord"* (2 Corinthians 3:18). Let us take hold of this promise as the possible and assured experience of daily life for everyone who gives Christ His place as the Glorified One. Let us keep our hearts set on the glory of the image of God in Christ, in the assurance that the Spirit will change us into that image day by day. Dear reader, take time to believe firmly and confidently that this promise will be made true in your Christian life. God Almighty, who created man in His image, seeks now to work out His purpose in changing you into the image of Christ Jesus by the power of the Holy Spirit.

> *Let this mind be in you, which was also in Christ Jesus.*
> (Philippians 2:5)

> *For I have given you an example, that ye should do as I have done to you.* (John 13:15)

— 2 —

THE OBEDIENCE OF FAITH

The LORD appeared to Abram, and said unto him,
I am the Almighty God; walk before me, and be thou perfect.
And I will...multiply thee exceedingly.
—Genesis 17:1–2

In Abraham, we see not only how God asks for and rewards faith, but also how He works faith by the gracious training that He gives. When God first called Abraham, He gave the great promise, *"In thee shall all families of the earth be blessed"* (Genesis 12:3). When Abraham reached the land of Canaan, God met him with the promise that the land would belong to him (verse 7). When he returned from battle, God again met him to renew the promise that his descendants would be numbered as the stars. (See Genesis 15:5.)

God sought to strengthen Abraham's faith before the birth of Isaac, so He said, *"Walk before me, and be thou perfect. And I will...multiply thee exceedingly."* Again in the plains of Mamre, God asked, *"Is any thing too hard for the LORD?"* (Genesis 18:14). God led Abraham step by step until his faith was perfected for full obedience in the sacrifice of Isaac. As *"by faith Abraham, when he was called to go out"* (Hebrews 11:8), so by faith, at the end of forty years, he was able, without any promise, to obey God's will to the very uttermost—even when it appeared to conflict with all His promises.

Children of Abraham, children of God, the Father makes great demands on your faith. If you are to follow in Abraham's footsteps, you too must forsake all and live in the land of spiritual promise, separated unto God, with nothing but His Word to depend on. For this you will need a deep and clear insight that the God who is working in you is the Almighty who works according to *"the exceeding greatness of his power to us-ward who believe"* (Ephesians 1:19).

Do not think that it is easy to live the life of faith. It requires a life of abiding in His presence all day long. Bow before God in humble worship, until He speaks to you: *"I am the Almighty God; walk before me, and be thou perfect. And I will…multiply thee exceedingly."* When Abraham heard this, he *"fell on his face: and God talked with him"* (Genesis 17:3). In this lies the secret birthplace of the power to trust God for everything that He promises.

We can only go out like Abraham when we are called to a life of true consecration to God. Walk in the footsteps of Abraham. Hide deep in your heart the testimony of God's Word: *"He…was strong in faith…being fully persuaded that, what [God] had promised, he was able also to perform"* (Romans 4:20–21).

— 3 —

THE LOVE OF GOD

*And thou shalt love the Lord thy God with all thine heart, and
with all thy soul, and with all thy might.*
—Deuteronomy 6:5

God taught Abraham what it was to believe in Him with all his
heart; therefore, he *"was strong in faith, giving glory to God"* (Romans
4:20). Moses taught Israel what the first and great commandment
was: to love God with their whole hearts. This was the first commandment, the fountain out of which the others naturally proceed. It
has its foundation in the relationship between God and man—God
as the loving Creator, and man made in His image as the object of
that love. It could never be otherwise.

Man finds his life, destiny, and happiness in only one thing:
loving God with all his heart and all his strength. Moses said, *"The
Lord had a delight in thy fathers to love them"* (Deuteronomy 10:15);
such a God was infinitely worthy of being loved. All our religion, all
our faith in God and obedience to Him, and our entire lives are to be
inspired by one thought: we are to love God with all our hearts and
all our strength. The first duty of the child of God every day is to live
out this command.

How seldom Israel was able to obey the command! But before
Moses died, after speaking of the judgments God would bring upon
His people for their sins, he was able to make known the promise:
*"And the Lord thy God will circumcise thine heart...to love the Lord thy
God with all thine heart, and with all thy soul"* (Deuteronomy 30:6), and

He will do it *"with the circumcision made without hands"* (Colossians 2:11), by the circumcision of Christ on the cross.

This blessed promise was the first indication of the new covenant. Jeremiah foretold of the law being written in their hearts by the Holy Spirit so that they would no longer depart from God but would walk in His ways. (See Jeremiah 31:33.) But how little have Christians understood this; how easily they rest content with the thought that it is impossible!

Learn the double lesson. A perfect heart, loving God with all your might, is what God claims, what He is infinitely worthy of, and what God Himself will give and work in you. Let your whole soul go out in faith to meet, wait for, and expect the fulfillment of this promise.

"The love of God is shed abroad in our hearts by the Holy Ghost which is given unto us" (Romans 5:5). That makes the grace of loving God with all our hearts most sure and blessed.

— 4 —

THE JOYFUL SOUND

Blessed is the people that know the joyful sound: they shall walk, O LORD, in the light of thy countenance. In thy name shall they rejoice all the day.
—Psalm 89:15–16

Good tidings of great joy" (Luke 2:10) was what the angel called the gospel message, which is called *"the joyful sound"* in Psalm 89. Such blessedness consists of God's people walking in the light of God and rejoicing in His name *"all the day."* Undisturbed fellowship and never-ending joy are their portion. In the Old Testament, such things were at times the experience of believers. But there was no continuance; the Old Testament could not secure it. Only the New Testament can and does give it.

In every well-ordered family, one finds the father delighting in his children, and the children rejoicing in their father's presence. This mark of a happy home on earth is what the heavenly Father has promised and delights to work in His people—walking in the light of His countenance and rejoicing in His name all day long. It has been promised; it has been made possible in Christ through the Holy Spirit filling the heart with the love of God. It is the heritage of every-one who is indeed seeking to love God with all his heart and with all his strength.

And yet, how many of God's children think it impossible and have even given up the hope and desire for a life of rejoicing in God's presence all day long! But Christ promised it so definitely: *"These things have I spoken unto you, that my joy might remain in you, and that your joy might be full*" (John 15:11); "*I will see you again, and your heart shall rejoice*" (John 16:22).

The Father wants His children to have perfect confidence in and love for Him. He knows their need for His presence every moment of the day for their happiness and strength. Christ maintains this life in us by the power of the Holy Spirit. Let us be content with nothing less than the blessedness of those who know the joyful sound: "*They shall walk…in the light of thy countenance. In thy name shall they rejoice all the day…For thou art the glory of their strength*" (Psalm 89:15–17).

The deeper we seek to enter into God's will for us, the stronger our faith will be that the Father can be content with nothing less than His child walking in the light of His countenance and rejoicing in His name all day long. We can be assured that what the Father has meant for us will be brought about in us through Christ and the Holy Spirit.

— 5 —

THE THOUGHTS OF GOD

For as the heavens are higher than the earth, so are…my
thoughts than your thoughts.
—Isaiah 55:9

In giving us His promises of what He will work in us, God reminds us that, as high as the heavens are above the earth, so high are His thoughts above ours—altogether beyond our power of spiritual understanding.

When He tells us that we are made in His image, that by grace we are actually renewed again into that image, and that as we gaze upon God's glory in Christ we are changed into the same image by the Spirit of the Lord, these are indeed thoughts higher than the heavens. When He told Abraham of all the mighty work He would do in him and his descendants, and through him in all the nations of the earth, this again is a thought higher than the heavens. Our human minds cannot take it in. When God calls us to love Him with all our hearts and promises to renew our hearts so that we will love Him with all our strength, here again is a thought out of the very heights of heaven. And when the Father calls us to a life in the light of His countenance and rejoicing in His name all day long, this is a gift out of the very depths of God's heart of love.

We ought to have deep reverence, humility, and patience while we are waiting for God by His Holy Spirit to impart to our hearts the life and light that can make us feel at home with these thoughts. We need daily, tender, abiding fellowship with God if we are ever to enter into His mind and have His thoughts make their home in us. What great faith is needed to believe that God not only will reveal the beauty and the glory of these thoughts, but also will so mightily work in us that their divine reality and blessing will fill our inmost beings!

Think of what Isaiah said, as quoted by Paul: *"Eye hath not seen, nor ear heard, neither have entered into the heart of man, the things which God hath prepared for them that love him. But God hath revealed them unto us by his Spirit"* (1 Corinthians 2:9–10). When Christ promised His disciples that the Holy Spirit would come from heaven to dwell with them, He said that the Spirit would fill us with the light and life of the heavenly world. In this way, Christ and the purposes of God—which are higher than the heavens are above the earth—were made their abiding experience. Dear reader, seek to realize that every day the Holy Spirit will fill your heart with the thoughts of God in all their heavenly power and glory.

THE NEW COVENANT IN JEREMIAH 31

I will make a new covenant with the house of Israel...I will put
my law in their inward parts, and write it in their hearts.
—Jeremiah 31:31, 33

When God made the first covenant with Israel at Sinai, He said, *"If ye will obey my voice indeed, and keep my covenant, then ye shall be a peculiar treasure unto me above all people"* (Exodus 19:5). But Israel, unfortunately, did not have the power to obey. Their whole nature was carnal and sinful. There was no provision in the covenant for the grace that would make them obedient. The law only served to show them their sin.

In Jeremiah 31, God promised to make a new covenant in which provision would be made to enable men to live a life of obedience. In this new covenant, the law was to be put in their minds and written in their hearts, *"not with ink, but with the Spirit of the living God"* (2 Corinthians 3:3), so that they could say with David, *"I delight to do thy will, O my God: yea, thy law is within my heart"* (Psalm 40:8). Through the Holy Spirit, the law and the people's delight in it would take possession of their inner lives. Or, as we see in Jeremiah 32:40, God would put His fear in their hearts so that they would not depart from Him.

In contrast to the Old Testament covenant, which made it impossible to remain faithful, this promise ensures a continual, wholehearted obedience as the mark of the believer who takes God at His Word and fully claims what the promise secures.

Learn the lesson well. In the new covenant, God's mighty power is shown in the heart of everyone who believes the promise, *"They shall not depart from me"* (Jeremiah 32:40). Bow in deep stillness before God, and believe what He says. The measure of our experience of this power of God, which will keep us from departing from Him, will always be in harmony with the law: *"According to your faith be it unto you"* (Matthew 9:29).

We need to make a great effort to keep the contrast between the Old and New Testaments very clear. The Old had a wonderful measure of grace, but not enough for continually abiding in the faith of obedience. But that is the definite promise of the New Testament: the power of the Holy Spirit leading the soul and revealing the fullness of grace to keep us *"unblameable in holiness"* (1 Thessalonians 3:13).

THE NEW COVENANT
IN EZEKIEL

Then will I sprinkle clean water upon you,
and ye shall be clean: from all your filthiness...I will put my
spirit within you, and cause you to walk in my statutes,
and ye shall keep my judgments.
—Ezekiel 36:25, 27

Here we find the same promise as in Jeremiah, the promise of being so cleansed from sin and being so renewed in the heart that there would be no doubt of walking in God's statutes and keeping His law. In Jeremiah, God had said, *"I will put my law in their inward parts"* (Jeremiah 31:33), and *"I will put my fear in their hearts, that they shall not depart from me"* (Jeremiah 32:40). Here in Ezekiel, He says, *"I will...cause you to walk in my statutes, and ye shall keep my judgments."* In contrast to the old covenant, in which there was no power to enable them to continue in God's law, the great mark of the new covenant would be a divine power enabling them to walk in His statutes and keep His judgments.

"Where sin abounded, grace did much more abound" (Romans 5:20), bringing about wholehearted allegiance and obedience. Why is this so seldom experienced? The answer is very simple: the promise is not believed, is not preached; its fulfillment is not expected. Yet how clearly it is laid out for us in a passage like Romans 8:1–4! In this passage, the man who had complained of the power *"bringing [him] into captivity to the law of sin"* (Romans 7:23) thanks God that he is now *"in Christ Jesus"* (Romans 8:1) and that the *"law of the Spirit of*

life in Christ Jesus hath made [him] *free from the law of sin and death"* (verse 2), so that the requirement of the law is fulfilled in all who walk after the Spirit (verse 4).

Once again, why are there so few who can give such testimony, and what is to be done to attain it? Just one thing is needed: faith in an omnipotent God who will, by His wonderful power, do what He has promised. *"I the Lord have spoken it, and will do it"* (Ezekiel 22:14). Oh, let us begin to believe that the promise will come true: *"Ye shall be clean: from all your filthiness...I will...cause you to walk in my statutes, and ye shall keep my judgments."* Let us believe all that God promises here, and God will do it. Beyond all power of thought, God has made His great and glorious promises dependent on our faith. And the promises will bring about more of that faith as we believe them. *"According to your faith be it unto you"* (Matthew 9:29). Let us put this truth to the test even now.

THE NEW COVENANT
AND PRAYER

*Call unto me, and I will answer thee, and show thee great and
mighty things, which thou knowest not.*
—Jeremiah 33:3

*I the LORD have spoken it, and I will do it.…I will yet for this
be enquired of by the house of Israel, to do it for them.*
—Ezekiel 36:36–37

The fulfillment of the great promises of the new covenant is dependent on prayer. In answer to the prayer of Jeremiah, God had said, *"I will put my fear in their hearts so that they will not depart from me"* (Jeremiah 32:40). And to Ezekiel, He had spoken, *"I will…cause you to walk in my statutes, and ye shall keep my judgments"* (Ezekiel 36:27). Because we are unbelieving and we judge the meaning of God's Word according to human thought and experience, there is no expectation of these promises being truly fulfilled. We do not believe that God means them to be literally true. We do not have the faith in the mighty power of God that is waiting to make His promise true in our experience.

And God has said that without such faith, our lives will be partial and limited. He has graciously pointed out the way in which such faith can be found; it is in the path of much prayer: *"Call unto me, and I will answer thee, and show thee great and mighty things, which thou knowest not."* Moreover, *"I will yet for this be enquired of by the house of Israel, to do it for them.*" When individual men and women turn to God with their whole hearts to plead these promises, He will fulfill them. It is in the exercise of intense, persevering prayer that faith will be strengthened to take hold of God and will surrender itself to His omnipotent working. Then, as one and another can testify of what God has done and will do, believers will help each other and will take their place as the church of the living God, pleading for and firmly expecting His promises to be fulfilled in larger measure. Then power will be given to them for the great work of preaching Christ in the fullness of His redemption to perishing men.

The state of the church, its members, our ministers, and our own hearts calls for unceasing prayer. We need to pray intensely and persistently that the need for the power of the Holy Spirit may be deeply felt and that a strong faith may be roused in the hearts of many to claim and to expect His mighty working. *"I the LORD have spoken it, and will do it"* (Ezekiel 22:14).

Lord, I believe; help thou mine unbelief. (Mark 9:24)

— 9 —

THE NEW COVENANT
IN HEBREWS

*For I will be merciful to their unrighteousness,
and their sins and their iniquities will I remember no more.*
—Hebrews 8:12

In Hebrews 8:6, Christ is called the *"mediator of a better covenant,
which was established upon better promises."* In Him, the two parts of
the covenant find their complete fulfillment.

First of all, He came to atone for sin, so that its power over
man was destroyed and free access to God's presence and favor was
secured. With that came the fuller blessing: the new heart, freed
from the power of sin, with God's Holy Spirit breathing into it the
delight in God's law and the power to obey it.

These two parts of the covenant can never be separated. And yet,
unfortunately, many people put their trust in Christ for the forgiveness of sin but never think of claiming the fullness of the promise
of being God's people and knowing Him as their God. They do not
allow God to bring into their experience a new heart cleansed from
sin, with the Holy Spirit breathing into it such love and delight in
God's law, and such power to obey, that they have access to the full
blessing of the new covenant.

Jesus Christ is *"the mediator of the new testament"* (Hebrews 9:15),
in which the forgiveness of sin is in the power of His blood, and in
which the law is written in hearts by the power of His Spirit. Oh, if

only we could understand that, just as surely as the complete pardon of sin is assured, so the complete fulfillment of the promises may be expected, too. *"I will put my fear in their hearts, that they shall not depart from me"* (Jeremiah 32:40); *"I will put my spirit within you, and cause you to walk in my statutes, and ye will keep my judgments"* (Ezekiel 36:27).

But God has said, *"Behold, I am the LORD, the God of all flesh: is there any thing too hard for me?"* (Jeremiah 32:27). He spoke these words to Jeremiah in regard to the new covenant. The new covenant requires strong, wholehearted desire for a life wholly given up to God. It means we must set aside all our preconceived opinions, and in faith believe in the mighty power of God. It means a surrender to Jesus Christ as *"the mediator of the new testament,"* a willingness to accept our place with Him, crucified to the world, to sin, and to self. It means a readiness to follow Him at any cost. Succinctly, the new covenant means a simple, wholehearted acceptance of Christ as Lord and Master—heart and life wholly His. God has said it and will do it. *"I the LORD have spoken it, and will do it"* (Ezekiel 22:14).

— 10 —

FAITH IN CHRIST

Ye believe in God, believe also in me.
—John 14:1

In the Lord's Farewell Discourses (John 14–17), when Christ was about to leave His disciples, He taught them that they were to believe in Him with the same perfect confidence with which they had rested in God. He said, *"Believe me that I am in the Father, and the Father in me.…He that believeth on me, the works that I do shall he do also"* (John 14:11–12). Here on earth, He had not been able to make Himself fully known to His disciples. But in heaven, the fullness of God's power would be His; He would, in and through His disciples, do greater things than He had ever done upon earth.

This faith must first of all focus itself on the person of Christ in His union with the Father. The disciples were to have perfect confidence that all that God had done could now be done by Jesus, too. The deity of Christ is the rock on which our faith depends. Christ as man, partaker of our nature, is indeed true God. As the divine power has worked in Christ even to the resurrection from the dead, so Christ can also, in His divine omnipotence, work in us all that we need.

Dear Christian, do you not see of what deep importance it is that you take time to worship Jesus in His divine omnipotence as one with the Father? That will teach you to depend on Him in His sufficiency to work in you all that you can desire. This faith must so possess you that every thought of Christ will be filled with the consciousness of His presence as an almighty Redeemer, able to save, sanctify, and empower you to the uttermost.

Child of God, bow in deep humility before this blessed Lord Jesus, and worship Him—*"My LORD and my God"* (John 20:28). Take time until you become fully conscious of an assured faith that Christ, as the almighty God, will work for you, in you, and through you all that God desires and all that you need. Let the Savior you have known and loved become as never before the mighty God. Let Him be your confidence and your strength.

In His farewell charge on the last night, the Savior began by telling His disciples that everything in their lives would depend on simply believing Him. By this, they would do greater things than He had ever done. At the close of His address, He repeated again, *"Be of good cheer; I have overcome the world"* (John 16:33). Our one need is a direct, definite, unceasing faith in the mighty power of Christ working in us.

CHRIST'S LIFE IN US

Because I live, ye shall live also.
—John 14:19

There is a great difference between the first three gospels and that of John. John was the beloved friend of Jesus. He understood the Master better than the others. John 13–17 is considered by many to be the inmost sanctuary of the New Testament. The other gospel writers spoke of repentance and the pardon of sin as the first great gift of the New Testament. But they said little of the new life that the new covenant was to bring, with the new heart in which the law had been put as a living power. John recorded what Christ taught about His life really becoming ours and our being united with Him just as He was with the Father. The other gospel writers spoke of Christ as the Shepherd seeking and saving the lost; John spoke of Him as the Shepherd who so gives His life for the sheep that His very life becomes theirs. *"I came that they may have life, and may have it abundantly"* (John 10:10 RV).

And so Christ said, "Because I live, you will live also." The disciples were to receive from Him, not the life He then had, but the resurrection life in the power of its victory over death and of His exaltation to the right hand of God. He would from then on always dwell in them; a new, heavenly, eternal life—the life of Jesus Himself—would fill them. And this promise is to all who will accept it in faith.

Unfortunately, so many people are content with the beginnings of the Christian life but never desire to have it in its fullness—the more abundant life. They do not believe in it; they are not ready for the sacrifice implied in being wholly filled with the life of Jesus. Child of God, the message comes again to you: *"The things which are impossible with men are possible with God"* (Luke 18:27). Take time and let Christ's wonderful promise possess your heart. Be content with nothing less than a full salvation, Christ living in you, and you living in Christ. Be assured that it is meant for everyone who will take time to listen to Christ's promises and believe that the almighty power of God will work in him the mighty wonder of His grace—Christ dwelling in the heart by faith.

— 12 —

THE OBEDIENCE OF LOVE

If ye keep my commandments, ye shall abide in my love;
even as I have kept my Father's commandments,
and abide in his love.
—John 15:10

Believers often ask, "How can I come to abide in Christ always, to live wholly for Him? Such is my desire and fervent prayer." In the above verse, the Lord gave the simple but far-reaching answer: *"Keep my commandments."* This is the only sure way, the blessed way, of abiding in Him. Loving obedience is the way to the enjoyment of His love.

The Lord spoke of this relationship between love and obedience on His last night. In John 14, we find it three times: *"If ye love me, keep my commandments"* (verse 15); *"He that hath my commandments, and keepeth them, he it is that loveth me: and he that loveth me shall be loved of my Father, and I will love him, and will manifest myself to him"* (verse 21); *"If a man love me, he will keep my words: and my Father will love him, and we will come unto him, and make our abode with him"* (verse 23). And chapter fifteen contains three more instances: *"If...my words abide in you, ye shall ask what ye will, and it shall be done unto you"* (verse 7); *"If ye keep my commandments, ye shall abide in my love"* (verse 10); and *"Ye are my friends, if ye do whatsoever I command you"* (verse 14). All six times, the Lord connected the keeping of the commandments with the promise of the great blessing that accompanies loving obedience—the indwelling of the Father and the Son in the heart. The love that keeps His commandments is the only way to abide in His love. In our relationship with Christ, love is everything—Christ's love for us, our love for Him, proved in our love for our fellow Christians.

How seldom believers have accepted this teaching! Many are content to think that it is impossible. They do not believe that through the grace of God, we can be kept from sin. They do not believe in the promise of the new covenant: *"I will put my spirit within you, and cause you to walk in my statutes, and ye shall keep my judgments"* (Ezekiel 36:27). They have no concept how, to a heart fully surrendered and given over to Him, Christ will make possible what otherwise appears beyond our reach: loving Him, keeping His commandments, and abiding in His love.

The wonderful promise of the Holy Spirit as the power of Christ's life in us is the pledge that we will indeed love Him and keep His words. This is the great secret of abiding in Christ, of having the indwelling of Christ and of God, and of the effectiveness of our prayers to bring God's blessing on all our work.

— 13 —

THE PROMISE OF THE SPIRIT

If I depart, I will send Him [the Holy Spirit] unto you.…He
shall glorify me: for he shall receive of mine,
and shall [show] it unto you.
—John 16:7, 14

The crucified Christ was to be glorified on the throne of heaven. Out of that glory He would send down the Holy Spirit into the hearts of His disciples to glorify Him in them. The Spirit of the crucified and glorified Christ would be their life in fellowship with Him, and their power for His service. The Spirit comes to us as the Spirit of divine glory; as such we are to welcome Him and yield ourselves absolutely to His leading.

"The Spirit searcheth all things, yea, the deep things of God" (1 Corinthians 2:10). The Spirit who dwells in the very roots of the Divine Being, who had been with Christ through His life and in His death upon the cross—this Spirit of the Father and the Son was to come and dwell in the disciples and make them the conscious possessors of the presence of the glorified Christ. It was this blessed Spirit who was to be their power for a life of loving obedience, to be their Teacher and Leader in praying down from heaven the blessing that they needed. And it was in His power that they were to conquer God's enemies and carry the gospel to the ends of the world.

It is this Spirit that the church lacks so sadly; it is this Spirit she grieves so unceasingly. It is owing to this spiritual poverty that her work is so often feeble and fruitless.

The Spirit is God. As God, He claims possession of our entire beings. We have too often thought of Him as our help in the Christian life, while we have not known that our hearts and lives are to be entirely and unceasingly under His control. Indeed, we are to be led by the Spirit every day and every hour. In His power, we are to directly and continually abide in the love and fellowship of Jesus. No wonder we have not believed in the great promise that in a love that keeps the commandments, we can always abide in Christ's love! No wonder we do not have the courage to believe that Christ's mighty power will work in us and through us! No wonder His divine prayer promises are beyond our reach! The Spirit who searches *"the deep things of God"* claims the very depths of our beings, so that He may there reveal Christ as Lord and Ruler.

The promise waits for its fulfillment in our lives: *"He shall glorify me: for he shall receive of mine, and shall* [show] *it unto you."* Let us yield ourselves today to believe the promise at once and with our whole hearts. Christ waits to make it true.

— 14 —

IN CHRIST

At that day ye shall know that I am in my Father,
and ye in me, and I in you.
—John 14:20

Our Lord spoke of His life in the Father: *"Believe me that I am in the Father, and the Father in me"* (verse 11). He and the Father were not two individuals next to each other; they were in each other. Though Christ was on earth as a man, He lived in the Father. Everything He did was what the Father did in Him.

This divine life of heaven, of Christ in God and of God in Christ, is the picture and the pledge of what our life in Christ is to be here on earth. It is in the very nature of the divine life that the Son is in the Father. Even so, we must know and ever live in the faith that we are in Christ. Then we will learn that, even as the Father worked in Christ, so Christ will also work in us if we only believe that we are in Him and yield ourselves to His power.

And even as the Son waited on the Father and as the Father worked through Him, so the disciples would make known to Him in prayer what they wanted done on earth, and He would do it. Their life in Him was to be the reflection of His life in the Father. As the Father worked in Him, because He lived in the Father, so Christ would work in them as they lived in Him.

But this would not be fulfilled until the Holy Spirit came. They had to wait until they were filled with the power from on high. For this they abided in Him by daily fellowship and prayer, so that He might do in them the greater works He had promised.

How little the church understands that the secret of her power is to be found in nothing less than where Christ found it, abiding in the Father and His love! Ministers, too, seldom understand that this should be their one great goal, daily and hourly to abide in Christ as the only possible way of being equipped and used by Him in the great work of winning souls to Him. If anyone asks what the lost secret of the pulpit is, we have it here: *"At that day"*—when the Spirit fills your heart—*"ye shall know that I am in my Father, and ye in me, and I in you."*

A PRAYER

Blessed Lord, teach us to surrender ourselves unreservedly to the Holy Spirit. Teach us, above everything, to wait daily for His teaching, so that we, too, may know the blessed secret, that as You are in the Father, so we are in You, and You work through us. Gracious Lord, pour down upon all Your children who are seeking to work for You, such a spirit of grace and of supplication that we may not rest until we, too, are filled with the Holy Spirit. Amen.

— 15 —

ABIDING IN CHRIST

Abide in me, and I in you.
—John 15:4

Using the parable of the vine and the branch, our Lord sought to enforce and illustrate what He had taught in John 14 concerning our union with Him and His union with the Father. He did this all for the sake of bringing home to the apostles and to all His servants in the gospel the absolute necessity of a life in daily full communion with Him. *"Abide in me."*

On the one hand, He pointed to Himself and to the Father and indicated, "Just as truly and fully as I am in the Father, so you are in Me." Then, pointing to the vine, He essentially said, "Just as truly as the branch is in the vine, you are in Me. Just as the Father abides in Me and works in Me; just as I work out what He works in Me; just as the branch abides in the vine, the vine gives its life and strength to the branch, and the branch receives it and puts it forth in fruit—even so do you abide in Me and receive My strength. With an almighty power, I will work My work in you and through you. Abide in me."

Dear child of God, you have often meditated on this blessed passage. But do you not feel that you still have much to learn in order to have Christ's almighty power working in you as He desires? The great need is to take time in waiting on the Lord Jesus in the power of His Spirit, until the two great truths get complete mastery of your being: Christ is in God, and you are in Christ.

Our Lord said, *"He that abideth in me, and I in him, the same bringeth forth much fruit"* (verse 5). Fruit is what Christ seeks; it is what He works and what He will assuredly give to the person who trusts Him.

To the feeblest of God's children, Christ says, "You are in Me. Abide in Me, and you will bear much fruit." To the strongest of His messengers, He still says, "Abide in Me, and you will bear much fruit." To one and all, the message comes: daily, continuous, unbroken abiding in Christ Jesus is the one condition of a life of power and blessing. Take time and let the Holy Spirit so renew in you the secret abiding in Him that you may understand the meaning of His words: *"These things have I spoken unto you, that my joy might remain in you, and that your joy might be full"* (verse 11).

The Lord asks us, "Do you believe that I can do this, that I can keep you abiding in My love?" And when we answer Him, "Yes, Lord," He tells us, *"Be not afraid, only believe"* (Mark 5:36).

— 16 —

THE POWER OF PRAYER

If ye abide in me, and my words abide in you,
ask whatsoever ye will, and it shall be done unto you.
—John 15:7 RV

Before our Lord went up to heaven, He taught His disciples two great lessons in regard to their relationship with Him in the great work they had to do. The one was that in heaven, He would have much more power than He had upon earth, and He would use that power for the salvation of men, solely through them, their words, and their work. The other lesson was that, without Him, they could do nothing, but they could depend on Him to work in them and through them, and so carry out His purpose. Their first and chief work would therefore be to bring everything they wanted done to Him in prayer. They knew and depended on His promise: *"Ask whatsoever ye will, and it shall be done unto you."*

With these two truths written in their hearts, He sent them out into the world. They could confidently undertake their work. The almighty, glorified Jesus was ready to do in and with and through them greater things than He Himself had ever done upon earth. The helpless disciples on earth unceasingly looked up to Him in prayer, with the full confidence that He would hear those prayers—but only on the condition that they have an unflinching confidence in the power of His promise. The chief thing in their lives and in their ministry was to be the maintenance of a spirit of prayer and supplication.

But how little the church has understood and believed this! Why? Simply because believers live so little in the daily abiding in Christ that they are powerless in believing His *great and precious promises* (2 Peter 1:4). Let us learn the lesson, both for our lives and our work, that as the members of Christ's body, the chief thing every day must be a close abiding fellowship with Christ that is based in deep dependence and unceasing supplication. Only then can we do our work in the full assurance that He has heard our prayers and will be faithful in doing His part—in giving the power from on high as the source of strength and abundant blessing. Take time, you *servants of the Lord* (Psalm 113:1), and with your whole hearts believe the word Christ has spoken. Christ asks, *"Believest thou this?...Yea, Lord: I believe"* (John 11:26–27). *"Continue ye in my love"* (John 15:9).

THE MYSTERY OF LOVE

That they all may be one; as thou, Father, art in me,
and I in thee....that they may be one, even as we are one:
I in them, and thou in me.
—John 17:21–23

During His last evening on earth, Christ especially pressed the thought of the disciples being in Him and abiding in Him. He also mentioned His being in them, but He did not emphasize this as much as their being in Him. But in His prayer as High Priest, He gave greater place to the thought of His being in them, just as the Father was in Him: *"And the glory which thou gavest me I have given them; that they may be one, even as we are one: I in them, and thou in me, that they may be made perfect in one; and that the world may know that thou hast sent me, and hast loved them, as thou hast loved me"* (verses 22–23).

The power to convince the world that God loved the disciples as He loved His Son could only come as believers lived their lives with Christ in them and proved it by loving their fellowmen as Christ loved them. The feebleness of the church is owing to the fact that we have not, by our example, proved to the world that our lives are in Christ and His life is in us. What is needed? Nothing less than a complete indwelling of Christ in the heart, and a binding together of believers because they know each other as those who have Christ dwelling in them. The last words of Christ's prayer in John 17 read, *"And I have declared unto them thy name, and will declare it: that the love wherewith thou hast loved me may be in them, and I in them"* (verse 26).

The divine indwelling has its chief glory in that it is the manifestation of divine love. It is the Father's love for Christ, brought by Christ to us, flowing out from us to all men.

Christ gave this great promise to every loving, obedient disciple: *"My Father will love him, and we will come unto him, and make our abode with him"* (John 14:23). It is to live this life of love for Christ and one's fellowmen that the Holy Spirit, in whom the Father and the Son are One, desires to live in our hearts. Let nothing less than this be what you seek, what you believe, and what you claim with your whole heart and strength—the indwelling of the Lord Jesus in the love *"which passeth knowledge"* (Ephesians 3:19), with which He can fill your heart. In this way, the world will be constrained by the love God's children have for each other to acknowledge that Christ's words are being fulfilled: *"That the love wherewith thou hast loved me may be in them, and I in them"* (John 17:26).

CHRIST OUR RIGHTEOUSNESS

Being justified freely by his grace through the
redemption that is in Christ Jesus.
—Romans 3:24

The first three gospel writers spoke of redemption as a pardon of sin, or justification. John spoke of it as a life that Christ is to live in us—a regeneration. In Paul's letters, however, we find both truths in beautiful harmony.

Paul first spoke of justification in Romans 3:21–5:11. Then he went on from 5:12 to 8:39 to speak of the life that is lived in union with Christ. In Romans 4, he told us that we find both these things in Abraham: *"Abraham believed God, and it was counted unto him for righteousness....To him that...believeth on him that justifieth the ungodly, his faith is counted for righteousness"* (verse 3, 5). Then, in verse 17, Abraham *"believed, even God, who quickeneth the dead."* Just as God considered Abraham's faith as righteousness and then led him on to believe in Him as the God who can give life to the dead, so it is with every believer.

Justification comes when the eye of faith is fixed on Christ. But that is only the beginning. Gradually the believer begins to understand that he was at the same time born again, that he has Christ in him, and that his calling now is to abide in Christ and let Christ live and work in him.

Most Christians strive, by holding on to their faith in justification, to stir themselves up and strengthen themselves for a life of gratitude and obedience. But they fail sadly because they do not know, do not in full faith yield themselves to Christ, to maintain His life in them. They have learned from Abraham the first lesson: to believe in God who *"justifieth the ungodly."* But they have not gone on to the second great lesson: to believe in God *"who quickeneth the dead"* and daily renews that life through Christ, who lives in them and in whose life alone there is strength and fullness of blessing. The Christian life must be *"from faith to faith"* (Romans 1:17). The grace of pardon is only the beginning; growing in grace leads on to the fuller insight and experience of what it means to be in Christ, to live in Him, and to *"grow up into him in all things, which is the head, even Christ"* (Ephesians 4:15).

— 19 —

CHRIST OUR LIFE

*Much more they which receive abundance of grace and of the
gift of righteousness shall reign in life by one, Jesus Christ.*
—Romans 5:17

*Likewise reckon ye also yourselves to be dead indeed unto sin,
but alive unto God through Jesus Christ our Lord.*
—Romans 6:11

Paul taught us that our faith in Christ as our righteousness is to be followed by our faith in Him as our life from the dead. He asked, *"Know ye not, that so many of us as were baptized into Jesus Christ were baptized into his death?"* (Romans 6:3). We were buried with Him and were raised from the dead with Him. Just as all of mankind died in Adam, so all believers in Christ actually died in Him. *"Our old man is crucified with him"* (verse 6); with Him we were raised from the dead (see Colossians 2:12); and now we are to consider ourselves as *"dead indeed unto sin, but alive unto God."*

Truly, just as the new life in us is a participation in and experience of the risen life of Christ, so our death to sin in Christ is also a spiritual reality. When we, by the power of the Holy Spirit, are enabled to see how we were really one with Christ in His death and in His resurrection, we will understand that in Him sin has no power over us. We present ourselves unto God as being *"alive from the dead"* (Romans 6:13).

The man who knows that he died in Christ and is now alive in Him can confidently depend on it that *"sin shall not have dominion over"* him (verse 14), not even for a single moment. *"Reckon ye also yourselves to be dead indeed unto sin, but alive unto God through Jesus Christ our Lord"* (verse 11). This is the true life of faith.

Just as we can only live in Christ and have Him live in us as we experience the full power of the Holy Spirit, so it is here. Paul said, *"For the law of the Spirit of life in Christ Jesus hath made me free from the law of sin and death"* (Romans 8:2), which, he had complained, had kept him in captivity. Then he added, *"That the righteousness of the law might be fulfilled in us, who walk not after the flesh, but after the Spirit"* (verse 4). Through the Spirit, we enter into the glorious liberty of the children of God.

Oh, that God might open the eyes of His children to see what the power is of Christ living in them for a life of holiness and fruitfulness, when they consider themselves *"dead indeed unto sin, but alive unto God through Jesus Christ."*

— 20 —

CRUCIFIED WITH CHRIST

I am crucified with Christ: nevertheless I live;
yet not I, but Christ liveth in me.
—Galatians 2:20

As in Adam we died and went out of the life and will of God into sin and corruption, so in Christ we are made partakers of a new spiritual death—a death out of sin and into the will and life of God. Such was the death Christ died; such is the death we are made partakers of in Him. To Paul, this was such a reality that he was able to say, "*I am crucified with Christ: nevertheless I live; yet not I, but Christ liveth in me.*" Dying with Christ had such power that Paul no longer lived his own life; instead, Christ lived His life in him. He had indeed died to the old nature and to sin and had been raised up into the power of the living Christ dwelling in him.

It was the crucified Christ who lived in Paul and made him a partaker of all that the cross had meant to Christ Himself. The very mind that was in Christ—who emptied Himself, took "*the form of a servant*" (Philippians 2:7), and "*humbled himself, and became obedient unto death*" (verse 8)—was at work in Paul because the crucified Christ lived in him. He lived as a crucified man.

Christ's death on the cross was His highest display of His holiness and victory over sin. The believer who receives Christ is made a partaker of all the power and blessing that the crucified Lord has won. As the believer learns to accept this by faith, he yields himself as crucified to the world and dead to its pleasure and pride, its lusts and self-pleasing. He learns that the mystery of the cross, as the crucified Lord reveals its power in him, opens the door into the fullest fellowship with Christ and the conformity to His sufferings. And so he learns, in the full depth of its meaning, what the Word has said: *"Christ crucified...the power of God, and the wisdom of God"* (1 Corinthians 1:23–24). He grows into a fuller understanding of the blessedness of daring to say, "I am crucified with Christ: nevertheless I live; yet not I, but Christ lives in me."

Oh, the blessedness and power of the God-given faith that enables a man to live all day yielding himself to God and considering himself as *"dead indeed unto sin, but alive unto God through Jesus Christ"* (Romans 6:11).

— 21 —

THE FAITH LIFE

The life which I now live in the flesh I live by the faith of the Son
of God, who loved me, and gave himself for me.
—Galatians 2:20

If we were able to ask Paul, "What is your part in living life, if you no longer live but Christ lives in you?" he would answer, "*The life which I now live in the flesh I live by the faith of the Son of God, who loved me, and gave himself for me.*" His whole life, day by day and all day long, was one of unceasing faith in the wonderful Love that had given itself for him. Faith was the power that possessed and permeated Paul's whole being and his every action.

Here we have the simple but full statement of the secret of the true Christian life. It is not faith that rests only in certain promises of God or in certain blessings that we receive from Christ. It is a faith that sees how entirely Christ gives Himself to the soul to be his entire life and all that implies for every moment of the day. Just as continuous breathing is essential to the support of our physical life, so is the unceasing faith in which the soul trusts Christ and depends on Him to maintain the life of the Spirit within us. Faith always rests on the infinite love in which Christ gave Himself wholly for us to be entirely ours and to live His life over again in us. By virtue of His divine omnipresence, by which He "*filleth all in all*" (Ephesians 1:23), He can be to each what He is to all—a complete and perfect Savior, an abiding Guest, taking charge and maintaining our life in us and for us—as if each of us were the only one in whom He lives. Just as truly as the

Father lived in Him and worked in Him all that He was to work out, so will Christ live and work in each one of us.

When our faith is led and taught by God's Holy Spirit, we obtain such a confidence in the omnipotence and omnipresence of Christ that we carry all day in the depths of our hearts this unbroken assurance: "He who loved me and gave Himself for me, lives in me; He is my life and my all. I can do all things through Christ, who strengthens me." May God reveal to us the inseparable union between Christ and us, in which the consciousness of Christ's presence may become as natural to us as the consciousness of our existence.

FULL CONSECRATION

*I count all things but loss for the excellency of the knowledge of
Christ Jesus my Lord.*
—Philippians 3:8

In studying the promises Jesus gave to His disciples during His last
night, the question arises: What was it that made these men worthy
of the high honor of being baptized with the Holy Spirit from heaven?
The answer is simple. When Christ called them, they forsook all and
followed Him. They denied themselves, even to the hating of their
own lives, and gave themselves to obey His commands. They followed
Him to Calvary, and amid its suffering and death, their hearts clung
to Him alone. It was this that prepared them for receiving a share in
His resurrection life, and so they were made ready to be filled with
the Spirit, even as Christ received the fullness of the Spirit from the
Father in glory.

Just as Jesus had to sacrifice all to be wholly an offering to God,
so all His people—from Abraham, Jacob, and Joseph to His twelve
apostles to today's believers—have had to give up all to follow the
divine leading, and have lived separated unto God, before the divine
power could fulfill God's purposes through them.

It was this way with Paul, too. To *count all things but loss for the
excellency of the knowledge of Christ Jesus my Lord*" was the keynote
of his life, as it must be in ours if we are to share fully in the power
of His resurrection. But how little the church understands that we
have been entirely redeemed from the world, to live wholly and only

for God and His love! As the merchant who found the treasure in the field had to sell all he had to purchase it, Christ claims the whole heart, the whole life, and the whole strength if we are indeed to share with Him in His victory through the power of the Holy Spirit. The law of God's kingdom is unchangeable; nothing compares to the excellence of the knowledge of Christ Jesus our Lord.

The disciples had to spend years with Christ in order to be prepared for Pentecost. Christ calls us to walk every day in the closest union with Him, to abide in Him without ceasing, and so to live as those who are not their own, but wholly His. In this life of full surrender, we will find the path to the fullness of the Spirit.

In faith, boldly believe that such a life is meant for you. Let your heart's fervent desire reach out for nothing less than this. Love the Lord and Christ your Savior with your whole heart. You will be "more than conquerors through him that loved us" (Romans 8:37).

— 23 —

ENTIRE SANCTIFICATION

The very God of peace sanctify you wholly; and I pray God…
[you be] blameless unto the coming of our Lord Jesus Christ.
Faithful is he that calleth you, who also will do it.
—1 Thessalonians 5:23–24

What a promise! One would expect to see all God's children clinging to it, claiming its fulfillment. But, unfortunately, unbelief does not know what to think of it, and only a few people consider it their treasure and joy.

"The very God of peace"—the peace that He made by the blood of the cross, the peace that passes all understanding and keeps our hearts and thoughts in Christ Jesus (see Philippians 4:7)—alone can and will do it. This God of peace Himself promises to sanctify us wholly, in Christ our sanctification, in the sanctification of the Spirit. It is God who is doing the work. It is in close, personal fellowship with God Himself that we become holy.

Should not all of us rejoice with exceeding joy at the prospect? But it is as if the promise is too great for many of us, and so it is repeated and amplified. May your spirit (the inmost part of your being, created for fellowship with God), your soul (the seat of the life and all its powers), and your body (through which sin entered and in which sin proved its power even unto death, but which has been redeemed in Christ)—may these be preserved whole, without blame, at the coming of our Lord Jesus Christ. (See 1 Thessalonians 5:23.)

To prevent the possibility of any misunderstanding, as if it is too great to be literally true, these words are added to our next verse: *"Faithful is he that calleth you, who also will do it."* Yes, God has said, *"I the LORD have spoken it, and I will do it"* (Ezekiel 36:36). He will do it in Christ and through the Holy Spirit. He asks only that we come and abide in close fellowship with Him every day. As the heat of the sun shines on the body and warms it, so the fire of His holiness will burn in us and make us holy.

Child of God, beware of unbelief. It dishonors God and robs your soul of its heritage. Take refuge in this: *"Faithful is he that calleth you, who also will do it."* Yes, He will do it, and He will give you grace to abide in His nearness so that you can always be under the cover of His perfect peace and of the holiness that He alone can give.

> *All things are possible to him that believeth....Lord, I believe; help thou mine unbelief.* (Mark 9:23–24)

24

THE EXCEEDING GREATNESS
OF HIS POWER

[I] cease not to…[make] mention of you in my prayers;
that the God of our Lord Jesus Christ, the Father of glory, may
give unto you the spirit of wisdom and revelation…
the eyes of your understanding being enlightened;
that ye may know…what is the exceeding greatness of his power
to us-ward who believe, according to the working of his mighty
power, which he wrought in Christ,
when he raised him from the dead.
—Ephesians 1:16–20

Here is one of the great Scriptures that will make our faith large, strong, and bold. Paul was writing to those who had been sealed with the Holy Spirit, yet he felt the need for unceasing prayer for the enlightening of the Spirit, so that they might truly know the mighty power of God that was working in them. It was nothing less than this very same power, the strength of His might, by which He raised Christ from the dead.

Christ died on the tree, weighed down by the sin of the world and its curse. When He descended into the grave, it was under the weight of all that sin and under the power of the death that had apparently mastered Him. What a mighty working of the power of God, to raise that Man out of the grave to the power and the glory of His throne! And now it is that same power, in its *"exceeding greatness…to us-ward who believe"* that we, by the teaching of the Holy Spirit, are to know as working in us every day of our lives. The God who said, *"I am the LORD…is there any thing too hard for me?"* (Jeremiah 32:27) comes to us with the message that what He did in Abraham and in Christ Jesus is the pledge of what He is doing every moment in our hearts and will complete if we learn to trust Him.

It is by that almighty power that the risen and exalted Christ can be revealed in our hearts as our life and our strength. How rarely Christians believe this! Oh, let us cry to God; let us trust God for His Holy Spirit to enable us to claim nothing less every day than the *"exceeding greatness"* of this resurrection power working in us!

Let us especially pray for all believers around us and throughout the church, that they may have their eyes opened to the wonderful vision of God's almighty resurrection power working in them. And let ministers, like Paul, make this a matter of continual intercession for those among whom they labor. What a difference it would make in their ministry—the unceasing prayer for the Spirit to reveal the power that dwells and works in them!

25

THE INDWELLING CHRIST

For this cause I bow my knees unto the Father of our Lord Jesus Christ…that he would grant you, according to the riches of his glory, to be strengthened with might by his Spirit in the inner man; that Christ may dwell in your hearts by faith; that ye, being rooted and grounded in love… might be filled with all the fulness of God.
—Ephesians 3:14, 16–17, 19

The great privilege that separated Israel from other nations was this: they had God dwelling in their midst; His home was in *"the Holiest of All"* (Hebrews 9:3).

The New Testament is the dispensation of the indwelling God in the hearts of His people. Christ said, *"If a man love me, he will keep my words: and my Father will love him, and we will come unto him, and make our abode with him"* (John 14:23). This is what Paul referred to as *"the riches of the glory of this mystery among the Gentiles; which is Christ in you, the hope of glory"* (Colossians 1:27). Or, as he said of himself, *"Christ liveth in me"* (Galatians 2:20). How few Christians experience this! Let us study Paul's teaching in Ephesians 3:14–19 on the way to experience this crowning blessing of the Christian life.

1. *"I bow my knees to the Father."* The blessing must come from the Father. It is to be found in much prayer.

2. *"That he would grant you, according to the riches of his glory"*—something very special and divine—*"to be strengthened with might through His Spirit in the inner man."* God

gives us the strength to be separate from sin and the world, to yield to Christ as Lord and Master, and to live the life of love for Christ and keeping His commandments to which the promise has been given that He will live in us. (See John 14:23.)

3. *"That Christ may dwell in your hearts by faith."* Christ, in His divine omnipresence and love, longs for hearts to dwell in. As a believer sees this by faith, bows his knee, and asks God for this great blessing, he receives grace to believe that the prayer is answered. And through that faith, he accepts the wonderful gift desired for so long—Christ dwelling in the heart by faith.

4. *"That ye, being rooted and grounded in love…might be filled with all the fullness of God,"* as far as it is possible for man to experience it.

Feed on the words the Holy Spirit has given here, and hold fast to the confident assurance that God will do *"abundantly above all that we ask or think"* (Ephesians 3:20).

26

CHRISTIAN PERFECTION

Now the God of peace…make you perfect in every good work to do his will, working in you that which is wellpleasing in his sight, through Jesus Christ.
—Hebrews 13:20–21

Prepare your heart, my reader, for a large and strong faith—a faith that takes hold of one of God's promises that are as high above all our thoughts as the heaven is above the earth. (See Isaiah 55:9.)

In the epistle to the Hebrews, we have a wonderful presentation of the eternal redemption that Christ our great High Priest, *"the mediator of the new testament"* (Hebrews 9:15), worked out for us through the shedding of His precious blood. The writer of the epistle closed his whole argument and all its deep spiritual teaching with the benediction, *"Now the God of peace…make you perfect in every good work to do his will."* Does that not include everything? Can we desire more? Yes, *"working in you that which is wellpleasing in his sight,"* and that through Jesus Christ.

The great thought here is that all that Christ had accomplished for our redemption, and all that God had done in raising Him from the dead, was done just with the one aim that He might now have more room to work in us the everlasting redemption that Christ brought in. He Himself, as God the Omnipotent, will make us *"perfect in every good work."* And if we want to know in what way, we have the answer: by His working within us *"that which is wellpleasing in his sight, through Jesus Christ."*

All that we have been taught about the completeness of the salvation in Christ and our call to follow Him here finds its consummation: we may be assured that God Himself takes such an entire charge of the man who really trusts Him, that He Himself will through Jesus Christ work all that *"is wellpleasing in his sight."*

The thought is too high; the promise is too large; we cannot attain it. And yet there it is, claiming, stimulating our faith. It calls us to take hold of the one truth that the everlasting God works in us every hour of the day *"through Jesus Christ."* We have just one thing to do: yield ourselves into God's hands for Him to work—not to hinder Him by our working, but in a silent adoring faith to be assured that He Himself through Jesus Christ will work in us all that *"is wellpleasing in his sight."*

Lord, *"Increase our faith"* (Luke 17:5)!

— 27 —

THE GOD OF ALL GRACE

The God of all grace, who hath called us unto his eternal glory
by Christ Jesus, after that ye have suffered a while, make you
perfect, stablish, strengthen, settle you.
—1 Peter 5:10

The book of Hebrews gathers up all its teaching in the wonderful promise: *"The God of peace…make you perfect in every good work"* (Hebrews 13:20–21). Peter did the same thing here: *"The God of all grace…perfect, establish, strengthen, [and] settle you."* God Himself is to be the one object of our trust every day; as we think of our work, our needs, our lives, and all our hearts' desires, God Himself must be the one object of our hope and trust.

Just as God is the center of the universe, the one source of its strength, the one Guide who orders and controls its movements, so God must have the same place in the life of the believer. With every new day, the first and chief thought ought to be, "God, God alone, can help me to live today as He wants me to live."

And what is to be our position toward this God? Should not our first thought every day be to humbly place ourselves in His hands, to confess our absolute helplessness, and to yield ourselves in childlike surrender to receive from Him the fulfillment of His promises— promises such as *"the God of peace… make you perfect in every good work"* (Hebrews 13:20–21), and *"The God of all grace…perfect, establish, strengthen, settle you"*?

It is absolutely indispensable to meet God every morning, give Him time to reveal Himself, and let Him take charge of your life for the day. Do we not have to do the same with these wonderful words of Peter? Yes, it must be understood between God and ourselves that our hearts are resting on Him, that our hope is in His Word, that the God of peace and all grace make us *"perfect in every good work,"* and *"establish, strengthen, settle"* us.

By His grace, may this henceforth be the spirit in which we awake every morning to go out to our work, humbly trusting in the promise that God Himself will perfect us: *"The LORD will perfect that which concerneth me"* (Psalm 138:8).

A PRAYER

Ever blessed Father, open the eyes of Your children to the vision that, even as Your Son was perfected forevermore, so You are waiting to work in each of us that work of perfecting Your saints in which Your glory will be seen. Amen.

NOT SINNING

*And ye know that he was manifested to take away our sins; and
in him is no sin.
Whosoever abideth in him sinneth not.*
—1 John 3:5–6

John had taken deep into his heart and life the words that Christ
had spoken on the last night—words about abiding in Him. He
always remembered how the Lord had spoken six times of loving
Him and keeping His commandments as the way to abide in His love
and receive the indwelling of the Father and the Son. And so, abiding
in Christ is one of the key promises in this epistle that he wrote in
his old age.

John taught how we can be kept from sinning: "*Whosoever abideth in him sinneth not.*" Though there is sin in our nature, the abiding
in Christ, in whom there is no sin, does indeed free us from the power
of sin and enable us to live daily so as to please God. The Scriptures
record that Christ had said of the Father, "*I do always those things
that please him*" (John 8:29). And so John wrote later in his epistle,
"*Beloved, if our heart condemn us not, then have we confidence toward
God. And whatsoever we ask, we receive of him, because we keep his commandments, and do those things that are pleasing in his sight*" (1 John
3:21–22).

Let the soul who longs to be free from the power of sin take hold
of these simple but far-reaching words: "*In him is no sin*" (verse 5).
God has established us in Christ. (See 2 Corinthians 1:21.) As you

seek to abide in our sinless Savior, Christ will indeed live out His own life in you in the power of the Holy Spirit and will equip you for a life in which you always do the things that are pleasing in His sight.

Dear child of God, you are called to a life in which faith in the almighty power of God—great faith that is strong, continuous, and unbroken—is your one hope. As you daily take time and yield yourself to the God of peace, who perfects you *"in every good work"* (Hebrews 13:21) to do His will, you will experience that God indeed works in those who wait for Him. (See Lamentations 3:25.)

"Whosoever abideth in him sinneth not." The promise is sure: God Almighty has pledged that He will work in you what is well-pleasing in His sight, through Christ Jesus. (See Hebrews 13:20–21.) In that faith, abide in Him.

> *Said I not unto thee, that, if thou wouldest believe, thou shouldest see the glory of God?* (John 11:40)

— 29 —

OVERCOMING THE WORLD

Who is he that overcometh the world,
but he that believeth that Jesus is the Son of God?
—1 John 5:5

Christ had spoken strongly about the world hating Him. His kingdom and the kingdom of this world were in deadly hostility. John had understood the lesson and summed it up in these words: "*And we know that we are of God, and the whole world lieth in wickedness*" (verse 19); "*Love not the world, neither the things that are in the world. If any man love the world, the love of the Father is not in him*" (1 John 2:15).

John also taught us that the real nature and power of the world is "*the lust of the flesh*" with its self-pleasing, "*the lust of the eyes*" that sees and seeks the glory of the world, "*and the pride of life*" with its self-exaltation (1 John 2:16). Eve in Paradise had these three marks of the world. She "*saw that the tree was good for food, and that it was pleasant to the eyes, and a tree to be desired to make one wise*" (Genesis 3:6). Through the body, the eyes, and the pride of wisdom, the world acquired mastery over her and over us.

The world still exerts a terrible influence over the Christian who does not know that, in Christ, he has been crucified to the world. (See Galatians 6:14.) The power of this world proves itself in the pleasure of eating and drinking, in the enjoyment of what is to be seen of its glory, and in all that constitutes the pride of life. Most Christians are either utterly ignorant of the danger of a worldly spirit, or they feel themselves utterly powerless to conquer it.

Christ left us with the great far-reaching promise: *"Be of good cheer; I have overcome the world"* (John 16:33). As the child of God abides in Christ and seeks to live the heavenly life in the power of the Holy Spirit, he may confidently depend on the power given him to overcome the world. *"Who is he that overcometh the world, but he that believeth that Jesus is the Son of God?"* (1 John 5:5). This is the secret of daily, hourly victory over the world and all its secret, subtle temptations: *"I live by the faith of the Son of God, who loved me, and gave himself for me"* (Galatians 2:20). But it needs a heart and a life entirely possessed by the faith of Jesus Christ to maintain the victor's attitude at all times. My fellow believer, take time to ask whether you believe with your whole heart in the victory that faith gives over the world. Put your trust in the mighty power of God, in the abiding presence of Jesus, as the only pledge of certain, continual victory.

— 30 —

JESUS: THE AUTHOR
AND FINISHER OF OUR FAITH

Lord, I believe; help thou mine unbelief.
—Mark 9:24

What a treasure of encouragement these words contain! Our Lord had said to the father of the possessed child, who had asked for His help, *"If thou canst believe, all things are possible to him that believeth"* (verse 23). The father felt that Christ was throwing the responsibility on him. If he believed, the child could be healed. But he felt as if he did not have such faith. As he looked in the face of Christ, he felt assured that the love that was willing to heal would also be ready to help with his faith and graciously accept even its feeble beginnings. And so he cried with tears, *"Lord, I believe; help thou mine unbelief."* Christ heard the prayer, and the child was healed.

What a lesson for us who have so often felt, as we listened to the wonderful promises of God, that our faith was too feeble to grasp the precious gift! Here we receive the assurance that the Christ who waits for our faith to do its work is the same Savior who will care for our faith. However feeble our faith may be, and though it comes with tears, let us cry, *"Lord, I believe; help thou mine unbelief."* Christ will accept the prayer that puts its trust in Him. Let us do this, even though our faith is *"as a grain of mustard seed"* (Matthew 17:20). In contact with Christ, the feeblest faith is made strong and bold. Jesus Christ is *"the author and finisher of our faith"* (Hebrews 12:2).

Dear Christian, as you read God's wonderful promises and long to have them fulfilled, remember the mustard seed. However small it may be, if it is put into the ground and allowed to grow, it becomes a great tree. Take the hidden, feeble seed of the little faith you have, and with the Word of promise on which you are resting, plant it in your heart. As it makes contact with Christ through fervent prayer to Him, He will accept the feeble, trembling faith that clings to Him without letting Him go. A feeble faith in an almighty Christ will become the great faith that can move mountains.

With Abraham, God took charge of his faith and trained him to become *"strong in faith, giving glory to God"* (Romans 4:20). You can confidently depend on Christ's desire to strengthen your faith. And when the question comes again, *"Believest thou this?"* (John 11:26), let your heart confidently say, *"Yea, Lord: I believe"* (verse 27). Praise God! Christ not only waits to give us the fullness of the heavenly life and the blessings of the covenant, but He also secretly works in us the faith that can claim it all.

— SECTION TWO —

THE SECRET OF THE CROSS

Jesus has now many lovers of His heavenly kingdom but few bearers of His cross. Many He has who are desirous of consolation but few of tribulation. Many He finds who share His table but few His fasting. All desire to rejoice with Him; few are willing to endure anything for Him. Many follow Jesus unto the breaking of bread but few to the drinking of the cup of His passion. Many reverence His miracles while few follow the shame of His cross.
—Thomas à Kempis[1]

The question often arises why, with so much churchgoing, Bible reading, and prayer, the Christian fails to live the life of entire sanctification and lacks the love and joy of the Lord. One of the most important answers undoubtedly is that he does not know what it is to die to himself and to the world. Without this, God's love and holiness cannot have their dwelling place in his heart. He has repented of some sins, but he does not know what it is to turn both from sin and from his old nature and self-will.

Yet this is what the Lord Jesus taught. He said to the disciples that if any man would follow Him, he must hate and lose his own life. (See Matthew 16:24–25; Luke 14:26.) He taught them each to take up his cross. That meant they were to consider their lives as sinful and under penalty of death. They were to give up themselves, their own wills and powers, and any goodness of their own. When their Lord

1. Thomas à Kempis, *Of the Imitation of Christ* (New Kensington, PA: Whitaker House, 1981).

had died on the cross, they would learn what it was to die to themselves and the world, and to live their lives in the fullness of God.

Our Lord used the apostle Paul to make this still clearer to us. Paul did not know Christ in the flesh, but through the Holy Spirit, Christ was revealed in his heart. Therefore, he could testify, *"I am crucified with Christ: nevertheless I live; yet not I, but Christ liveth in me"* (Galatians 2:20). In more than one of his epistles, the truth is made clear that we are dead to sin with Christ; each day, we receive and experience the power of the new life through the continual working of God's Spirit in us.

As the Easter season approaches each year, our thoughts are occupied with the sufferings and death of our Lord. Sermons once again emphasize Christ's death for us on the cross as the foundation of our salvation. But less is said about our death with Christ. The subject is a deep and difficult one, yet every Christian needs to consider it. It is my earnest desire to help those Christians who are considering this great truth, that death to self and to the world is necessary for a life in the love and joy of Christ.

I have sought to explain the words of our Lord and of His disciples on this subject. Allow me to point out two more things. First, take time to read over what you do not immediately understand. Spiritual truth is not easy to grasp. But experience has taught me that God's words, taken into the heart and meditated on with prayer, gradually help the soul to understand the truth. Secondly, be assured that only through the continual teaching of the Holy Spirit in your heart will you be able to take hold of spiritual truths. The great work of the Holy Spirit is to reveal Christ in our hearts and lives as the Crucified One who dwells within us. Let this be the chief aim of all your devotion: complete dependence on God and an expectation of continually receiving all goodness and salvation from Him alone. In this way, you will learn to die to yourself and to the world; you will receive Christ, the Crucified and Glorified One, into your heart; and you will be kept by the continual working of the Holy Spirit.

Let us pray fervently for each other, that God may teach us what it is to die with Christ—a death to ourselves and to the world, and a life in Christ Jesus.

A PRAYER

Heavenly Father, how can I thank You for the unspeakable gift of Your Son on the cross? How can I thank You for our eternal salvation, worked out by that death on the cross? He died for me so that I might live eternally. Through His death on the cross, I am dead to sin and live in the power of His life. Father in heaven, teach me what it means that I am dead with Christ and can live my life in Him. Teach me to realize that my sinful flesh is wholly corrupt and nailed to the cross to be destroyed, so that the life of Christ may be manifested in me. Teach me, above all, to believe that I cannot either understand or experience this except through the continual working of the Holy Spirit dwelling within me. Father, for Christ's sake, I ask it. Amen.

31

THE REDEMPTION OF
THE CROSS

Christ hath redeemed us from the curse of the law,
being made a curse for us.
—Galatians 3:13

Scripture teaches us that there are two points of view from which we may regard Christ's death upon the cross. One is the redemption of the cross: Christ dying for us as our complete deliverance from the curse of sin. The other is the fellowship of the cross: Christ taking us up to die with Him and making us partakers of the fellowship of His death.

In the verse from Paul's epistle to the churches of Galatia, we find three great unsearchable thoughts. First, the law of God has pronounced a curse on all sin and on all that is sinful. Second, Christ took our curse upon Him and even became a curse, thereby destroying its power. Third, in the cross, we now have the everlasting redemption from sin and all its power. The cross reveals to us that man's sin is under the curse, that Christ became a curse and overcame it, and that He is our full and everlasting deliverance from the curse.

In these thoughts, the most lost and hopeless sinner may find a sure ground of confidence and hope. In Paradise, God had indeed pronounced a curse on this earth and all that belongs to it. (See Genesis 3:17–19.) On Mount Ebal, in connection with giving the law, half of the people of Israel were twelve times over to pronounce a curse on all sin. (See Deuteronomy 27:11–26.) And there was to be in their midst a continual reminder of it: *"He that is hanged is accursed of God"* (Deuteronomy 21:23). And yet, who could ever have thought that the Son of God Himself would die on the accursed tree and become a curse for us? But such is the gospel of God's love, and the penitent sinner can now rejoice in the confident assurance that the curse is forever put away from all who believe in Christ Jesus.

The preaching of the redemption of the cross is the foundation and center of the salvation the gospel brings us. To those who believe its full truth, it is a cause of unceasing thanksgiving. It gives us boldness to rejoice in God. There is nothing else that will keep the heart as tender toward God, enabling us to live in His love and to make Him known to those who have never yet found Him. God be praised for the redemption of the cross!

32

THE FELLOWSHIP OF
THE CROSS

Let this mind be in you, which was also in Christ Jesus.
—Philippians 2:5

Paul told us here of the mind that was in Christ: He emptied Himself; He took the form of a servant; He humbled Himself, *"even* [to] *the death of the cross"* (verse 8). It is this mind that was in Christ— the deep humility that gave up His life to the very death—that is to be the spirit that animates us. In this way, we will prove and enjoy the blessed fellowship of His cross.

The Comforter had come to reveal His real presence in the Philippians. Paul said to them, *"If there be therefore any consolation in Christ...if any fellowship of the Spirit"* (verse 1), they were to breathe the Spirit of the crucified Christ and manifest His disposition in the fellowship of the cross in their lives.

As they strove to do this, they would feel the need of a deeper insight into their real oneness with Christ. They would learn to appreciate the truth that they had been crucified with Christ, that their *"old man"* (Romans 6:6) had been crucified, and that they had died to sin in Christ's death and were now living to God in His life. They would learn to know what it meant that the crucified Christ lived in them, that they had *"crucified the flesh with the affections and lusts"* (Galatians 5:24). Because the crucified Jesus lived in them, they could live crucified to the world.

And so they would gradually enter more deeply into the meaning and power of their high calling to live as those who were dead to sin, the world, and self. Each in his own measure would bear the marks of the cross, with its sentence of death on the flesh, with its hating of the self-life and its entire denial of self, and with its growing conformity to the crucified Redeemer in His deep humility and entire surrender of His will to the life of God.

This is a difficult thing to learn; there is no quick lesson in this school of the cross. But the personal experience of the fellowship of the cross will lead to a deeper understanding and a higher appreciation of the redemption of the cross.

— 33 —

CRUCIFIED WITH CHRIST

I am crucified with Christ: nevertheless I live;
yet not I, but Christ liveth in me.
—Galatians 2:20

The thought of fellowship with Christ in bearing His cross has often led to the futile attempt to follow Him and bear His image in our own power. But this is impossible for man until he first learns to know what it means to say, *"I am crucified with Christ."*

Let us try to understand this. When Adam died, all his descendants died with him and in him. You and I had a share in his sin in Paradise and in the spiritual death into which he fell; we died in him. And the power of that sin and death, in which all his descendants share, works in every child of Adam every day.

Christ came as the second Adam. All who believe in Him have a share in His death on the cross. Each one may say in truth, *"I am crucified with Christ."* As the representative of His people, He took them up with Him on the cross. This includes you and me. The life that He gives is the crucified life in which He entered heaven and was exalted to the throne, standing as *"a Lamb as it had been slain"* (Revelation 5:6). The power of His death and life does its work in us. As we hold fast the truth that we have been crucified with Him, and that now we no longer live, but Christ lives in us, we receive power to conquer sin. The life that we have received from Him is a life that has been crucified and made free from the power of sin.

This is a deep and very precious truth. Most Christians have little knowledge of it. This knowledge is not gained easily or speedily. It requires a great desire to be dead to all sin. It requires a strong faith, given by the Holy Spirit, so that the union with the crucified Christ and the fellowship of His cross can each day become our life. The life that He lives in heaven has its strength and its glory in the fact that it is a crucified life. And the life that He imparts to the believing disciple is a crucified life with its victory over sin and its power of access into God's presence.

It is indeed true that *"nevertheless I live; yet not I, but Christ liveth in me."* As we realize this by faith and hold fast the fact that the crucified Christ lives in us, life in the fellowship of the cross becomes a possibility and a blessed experience.

— 34 —

CRUCIFIED TO THE WORLD

But God forbid that I should glory, save in the
cross of our Lord Jesus Christ, by whom the world is
crucified unto me, and I unto the world.
—Galatians 6:14

What Paul had written in Galatians 2 is here confirmed at the end of the epistle and is expressed even more strongly. He insisted that his only glory was that, in Christ, he had been crucified to the world and entirely delivered from its power. When he said, *"I am crucified with Christ"* (Galatians 2:20), it was not only an inner spiritual truth, but also an actual, practical experience in relation to the world and its temptations.

Christ had spoken about the world hating Him and about His having overcome the world. Paul knew that the world that had nailed Christ to the cross had in that deed done the same to him. He boasted that he lived as one who had been crucified to the world, and the world as a powerless enemy was now crucified to him. It was this that made him glory in the cross of Christ. It had brought him complete deliverance from the world.

How very different is the relationship of Christians to the world today! They acknowledge that they must not commit the sins that the world allows. But still they are good friends with the world, and they feel free to enjoy as much of it as they can, if they only stay away from open sin. They do not know that the most dangerous source of sin is the love of the world with its lusts and pleasures.

Dear Christian, when the world crucified Christ, it crucified you with Him. When Christ overcame the world on the cross, He made you an overcomer, too. He calls you now, at whatever cost of self-denial, to regard the world, in its hostility to God and His kingdom, as a crucified enemy over whom the cross can ever keep you a conqueror.

The Christian who has learned to say by the Holy Spirit, *"I am crucified with Christ...[the crucified] Christ liveth in me"* (Galatians 2:20), has a very different relationship to the pleasures and attractions of the world. Let us ask God fervently that the Holy Spirit, through whom Christ offered Himself on the cross, may reveal to us in power what it means to *"glory...in the cross of our Lord Jesus Christ, by whom the world is crucified unto me."*

THE FLESH CRUCIFIED

And they that are Christ's have crucified the flesh
with the affections and lusts.
—Galatians 5:24

Concerning the flesh Paul taught us, *"In me (that is, in my flesh,)*
dwelleth no good thing" (Romans 7:18). And again he said, *"The carnal*
mind [the mind of the flesh] *is enmity against God: for it is not subject*
to the law of God, neither indeed can be" (Romans 8:7). When Adam
lost the Spirit of God, he became ruled by the flesh. *"The flesh"* is the
expression for the evil corrupt nature that we inherit from Adam. Of
this flesh, it is written, *"Our old man is crucified with him"* (Romans
6:6). And here Paul put it even more strongly: *"And they that are*
Christ's have crucified the flesh."

When the disciples heard and obeyed the call of Jesus to follow
Him, they honestly meant to do so, but as He later taught them what
that would imply, they were far from being ready to yield immediate
obedience. Likewise, those who are Christ's and have accepted Him
as the Crucified One scarcely understand what that includes. By their
act of surrender, they actually have crucified the flesh and consented
to regard it as an accursed thing, nailed to the cross of Christ.

But unfortunately, many Christians have never for a moment
thought of such a thing! It may be that the preaching of Christ crucified has been defective. It may be that the truth of our being crucified with Christ has not been taught. They shrink back from the

self-denial that it implies, and as a result, where the flesh is allowed in any measure to have its way, the Spirit of Christ cannot exert His power.

Paul taught, *"Walk in the Spirit, and ye shall not fulfil the lust of the flesh"* (Galatians 5:16); *"For as many as are led by the Spirit of God, they are the sons of God"* (Romans 8:14). The Spirit alone can guide us as the flesh, in living faith and fellowship with Christ Jesus, is kept in the place of crucifixion.

A PRAYER

Blessed Lord, how little I understood when I accepted You in faith that I once and for all *"crucified the flesh with the affections and lusts"*! I humbly ask You, teach me to believe and to live in You, the Crucified One, in such a way that, like Paul, I may always glory in the cross on which the world and the flesh are crucified. Amen.

— 36 —

BEARING THE CROSS

And he that taketh not his cross, and followeth after me,
is not worthy of me....
He that loseth his life for my sake shall find it.
—Matthew 10:38–39

Thus far we have looked at some of Paul's words to the Galatians about the cross and our being crucified with Christ. Let us now turn to the Master Himself to see what He has to teach us. We find that what Paul could teach openly and fully after the crucifixion was given by the Master in words that could at first hardly be understood and yet contained the seed of the full truth.

It was when Christ sent forth His disciples that He first used the expression that the disciple must take up his cross and follow Him. The only meaning the disciples could attach to these words was from what they had often seen, when an evildoer who had been sentenced to death by the cross was led out, bearing his cross, to the place of execution. In bearing the cross, the criminal acknowledged the sentence of death that was on him.

Christ wanted His disciples to understand that their natures were so evil and corrupt that only by losing their natural lives could they find true life. Of Himself, it was true: all His life, He bore His cross, the sentence of death that He knew was resting upon Him on account of our sins. And so He wants each of His disciples to bear his own cross, the sentence of death that is on himself and on his evil, carnal nature.

The disciples could not understand all this right away. But Christ gave them words that would germinate in their hearts like seeds and later begin to reveal their full meaning. Each disciple of Christ was not only to carry the sentence of death in himself, but also to learn that in following the Master to His cross, he would find the power to lose his life and receive instead the life that would come through the cross of Christ.

Christ asks His disciples to forsake all and take up their crosses, to give up their whole wills and lives, and to follow Him. The call comes to us, too, to give up the self-life with its self-pleasing and self-exaltation, and to bear the cross in fellowship with Him. In this way, we will be made partakers of His victory.

— 37 —

SELF-DENIAL

If any man will come after me, let him deny himself,
and take up his cross, and follow me.
—Matthew 16:24

For the first time, Christ had definitely announced that He would have to suffer much, be killed, and be raised again. "*Then Peter took him, and began to rebuke him, saying, Be it far from thee, Lord: this shall not be unto thee*" (verse 22). Christ's answer was, "*Get thee behind me, Satan*" (verse 23). The spirit of Peter, seeking to turn Him away from the cross and its suffering, was nothing but Satan tempting Him to turn aside from the path that God had appointed as our way of salvation.

Christ then added the words of our text verse, in which He used the words "*take up his cross*" for the second time. But with these words, He used a very significant expression revealing what is implied: "*If any man will come after me, let him deny himself.*" When Adam sinned, he fell out of the life of heaven and God and into the life of the world and self. Self-pleasing, self-sufficiency, and self-exaltation became the laws of his life. When Jesus Christ came to restore man to his original place, "*He humbled himself, and became obedient unto death, even the death of the cross*" (Philippians 2:8). What He has done Himself He asks of all who desire to follow Him: "*If any man will come after me, let him deny himself.*"

Instead of denying himself, Peter denied his Lord: "*I do not know the man*" (Matthew 26:72). When a man learns to obey Christ's commands, he says of himself, "I do not know the man!" The secret of true discipleship is to bear the cross, acknowledge the death sentence that has been passed on self, and deny any right that self has to rule over us.

Death to self—such is to be the Christian's watchword. The surrender to Christ is to be so entire, the surrender to live for those around us so complete, that self is never allowed to come down from the cross to which it has been nailed, but is always kept in the place of death.

Listen to the voice of Jesus and deny yourself. Let us ask God that we, as the disciples of Christ, who denied Himself for us, may by the grace of the Holy Spirit always live as those in whom self has been crucified with Christ and in whom the crucified Christ now lives as Lord and Master.

— 38 —

HE CANNOT BE MY DISCIPLE

*If any man come to me, and hate not...his own life also, he
cannot be my disciple. And whosoever doth not bear his cross,
and come after me, cannot be my disciple.....
So likewise, whosoever he be of you that forsaketh not all that he
hath, he cannot be my disciple.*
—Luke 14:26–27, 33

For the third time, Christ spoke here about bearing the cross. He gave new meaning to it when He said that a man must hate his own life and forsake all that he has. Three times, He solemnly repeated the words that without this, a man cannot be His disciple.

If a man *"hate not...his own life"*—why does Christ make such an exacting demand the condition of discipleship? Because the sinful nature we have inherited from Adam is indeed so vile and full of sin that if our eyes were only opened to see it in its true nature, we would flee from it as loathsome and incurably evil. The flesh is *"enmity against God"* (Romans 8:7); the soul that seeks to love God cannot help hating the *"old man"* (Romans 6:6) that is corrupt through its whole being. Nothing less than this, the hating of our own lives, will make us willing to bear the cross and carry within us the sentence of death on our evil natures. Not until we hate this life with a deadly hatred will we be ready to give up the old nature to die the death that is its due.

Christ added one more thing: whoever does not forsake all that he has, whether in property or character, *"cannot be my disciple."* Christ claims all. Christ undertakes to satisfy every need and to give a hundredfold more than we give up. When we by faith become conscious of what it means to know Christ, to love Him, and to receive from Him what can enrich and satisfy our immortal spirits, then we will regard as our highest privilege the surrender that at first appeared so difficult. As we learn what it means that Christ is our life, we will *"count all things but loss for the excellency of the knowledge of Christ Jesus* [our] *Lord"* (Philippians 3:8). In the path of following Him and always learning to know and love Him better, we willingly sacrifice all—including self with all its life—to make room for Him who is more than all.

— 39 —

FOLLOW ME

Then Jesus beholding him loved him, and said unto him,
One thing thou lackest: go thy way, sell whatsoever thou hast,
and give to the poor, and thou shalt have treasure in heaven:
and come, take up the cross, and follow me.
—Mark 10:21

When Christ spoke these words to the young rich man, he went away grieved. Jesus said, *"How hardly shall they that have riches enter into the kingdom of God!"* (verse 23). The disciples were astonished at His words. When Christ repeated once again what He had said, they were astonished beyond measure. *"Who then can be saved? And Jesus looking upon them saith, With men it is impossible, but not with God: for with God all things are possible"* (verses 26–27).

Christ had spoken about bearing the cross as the one condition of discipleship. This is the human side. Here with the rich young ruler, He revealed from the side of God what is needed to give men the will and the power to sacrifice all in order to enter the kingdom. He said to Peter, when he had confessed Him as Christ, the Son of God, that *"flesh and blood"* (Matthew 16:17) had not revealed it to him, but his Father in heaven. This was to remind Peter and the other disciples that it was only by divine teaching that he could make this confession. Likewise, with the young ruler, He unveiled the great mystery that it is only by divine power that a man can take up his cross, lose his life, deny himself, and hate the life to which he is by nature so attached.

Multitudes have sought to follow Christ and obey His command yet have found that they have utterly failed. Multitudes have felt that Christ's claims were beyond their reach and have sought to be Christians without any attempt at the wholehearted devotion and the entire self-denial that Christ seeks.

In our study of what the fellowship of the cross means, let us take today's lesson to heart. Let us believe that only by putting our trust in the living God and the mighty power in which He is willing to work in the heart can we attempt to be disciples who forsake all and follow Christ in the fellowship of His cross.

— 40 —

A GRAIN OF WHEAT

*Verily, verily, I say unto you, Except a [grain] of wheat fall into
the ground and die, it abideth alone; but if it die,
it bringeth forth much fruit. He that loveth his life lose it;
and he that hateth his life in this world shall
keep it unto life eternal.*
—John 12:24–25

All nature is the parable of how the losing of a life can be the way of securing a truer and a higher life. Every grain of wheat, every seed throughout the world, teaches the lesson that through death lies the path to beautiful and fruitful life.

It was so with the Son of God. He had to pass through death in all its bitterness and suffering before He could rise to heaven and impart His life to His redeemed people. And here, under the shadow of the approaching cross, He called His disciples: "If any man will serve Me, let him follow Me." (See Matthew 16:24.) He repeated the words: "*He that hateth his life in this world shall keep it unto life eternal.*"

One might have thought that Christ did not need to lose His holy life before He could find it again. But so it was: "*The Lord hath laid on him the iniquity of us all*" (Isaiah 53:6), and He yielded to the inexorable law that through death comes life and fruit.

How much more should we, in the consciousness of that evil nature and the death that we inherited in Adam, be most grateful that there is a way open to us by which, in the fellowship of Christ and His cross, we can die to this accursed self! With what gratitude we should listen to the call to bear our cross, to yield our *"old man"* (Romans 6:6) as crucified with Christ daily to the death that he deserves! Surely the thought that the power of eternal life is working in us ought to make us willing and glad to die the death that brings us into the fellowship and the power of life in a risen Christ.

Unfortunately, this is rarely understood. Let us believe that what is impossible to man is possible to God. (See Matthew 19:26.) Let us believe that the law of the Spirit of Christ Jesus, the Risen Lord, can indeed make His death and His life the daily experience of our souls.

— 41 —

YOUR WILL BE DONE

O my Father, if it be possible, let this cup pass from me:
nevertheless not as I will, but as thou wilt.
—Matthew 26:39

The death of Christ on the cross is the highest and holiest thing that can be known of Him even in the glory of heaven. And the highest and holiest thing that the Holy Spirit can work in us is to take us up and keep us in the fellowship of the cross of Christ. We need to enter deeply into the truth that Christ, the beloved Son of the Father, could not return to the glory of heaven until He had first given Himself over to death. As this great truth opens up to us, it will help us to understand how in our lives and in our fellowship with Christ, it is impossible for us to share His life until we have first surrendered ourselves every day to die to sin and the world, and so to abide in unbroken fellowship with our crucified Lord.

From Christ alone we can learn what it means to have fellowship with His sufferings and be *"conformed unto his death"* (Philippians 3:10 RV). In the agony of Gethsemane, when He looked toward what a death on the cross would be, He got such a vision of what it meant to die the accursed death under the power of sin, with God's face turned from Him so that not a single ray of its light could penetrate the darkness, that He prayed that the cup might pass from Him. But when no answer came and He understood that the Father could not allow the cup to pass by, He yielded up His whole will and life: *"Thy will be done"* (Matthew 26:42).

Dear Christian, in these words of your Lord in His agony, you can enter into fellowship with Him. In His strength, your heart will be made strong to believe most confidently that God in His omnipotence will enable you to yield up everything, because you have been crucified with Him.

"Thy will be done." Let this be the deepest and highest word in your life. In the power of Christ, with whom you have been crucified, and in the power of His Spirit, the definite daily surrender to the ever-blessed will of God will become the joy and strength of your life.

— 42 —

THE LOVE OF THE CROSS

Then said Jesus, Father, forgive them;
for they know not what they do.
—Luke 23:34

Christ's words on the cross—*"They know not what they do"*—reveal His mind and show what the minds of His disciples should be. Three words express Christ's wonderful love: *"Father, forgive them."* Christ prayed for His enemies. In the hour of their triumph over Him, in the hour of shame and suffering that they delighted in showering on Him, He poured out His love in prayer for them. The call to everyone who believes in a crucified Christ is to go and do likewise, even as He said:

> *Love your enemies, bless them that curse you, do good to them that hate you, and pray for them which despitefully use you, and persecute you.*   (Matthew 5:44)

The law of the Master is the law for every disciple; the love of the crucified Jesus is the only rule for those who believe in Him.

The love that cared for His enemies also cared for His friends. Jesus felt what the anguish must be in the heart of His widowed mother and so committed her to the care of the beloved disciple: *"Woman, behold thy son!...Behold thy mother!"* (John 19:26–27). Jesus knew that for John there could be no higher privilege and no more blessed service than that of taking His place in the care of Mary. Similarly, we who are the disciples of Christ must not only pray for

His enemies, but must also prove our love to Him and to all who belong to Him by making sure that every person is comforted and every loving heart has some work to do in caring for those who belong to the blessed Master.

"*Verily I say unto thee, Today shalt thou be with me in paradise*" (Luke 23:43). The penitent thief had appealed to Christ's mercy to remember him. With what readiness of joy and love Christ gave the immediate answer to his prayer! Whether it was the love that prayed for His enemies, the love that cared for His friends, or the love that rejoiced over the penitent sinner who was being cast out by man— in all these, Christ proved that the cross is a cross of love, that the Crucified One is the embodiment of a love that "*passeth knowledge*" (Ephesians 3:19).

With every thought of what we owe to that love, with every act of faith in which we rejoice in its redemption, let us prove that the mind of the crucified Christ is our mind, and that His love is not only what we trust in for ourselves, but also what guides us in our loving fellowship with the world around us.

— 43 —

THE SACRIFICE OF THE CROSS

My God, my God, why hast thou forsaken me?
—Matthew 27:46

I thirst....It is finished.
—John 19:28, 30

These words spoken on the cross reveal love in its outflow to men and in the tremendous sacrifice that it brought to deliver us from our sins and give the victory over every foe. They reveal the mind that was in Christ, which is to be the disposition of our whole lives.

"*My God, my God, why hast thou forsaken me?*" How deep must have been the darkness that overshadowed Him, when not one ray of light from the Father shone upon Him and He could not say, "My Father"! It was this awful desertion, breaking in upon that life of childlike fellowship with the Father in which He had always walked, that caused Him the agony and the bloody sweat in Gethsemane. "*O my Father, if it be possible, let this cup pass from me*" (Matthew 26:39). But He knew it could not pass away, so He bowed His head in submission: "*Thy will be done*" (verse 42). His love for God and for man caused Him to yield Himself to the very uttermost. As we learn to believe and worship that love, we, too, will learn to say, "*Thy will be done.*"

"*I thirst.*" The body of Christ here gave expression to the terrible experience of what it passed through when the fire of God's wrath against sin came upon Him in the hour of His desertion. He had spoken of the rich man crying out, "*I am tormented in this flame*" (Luke 16:24). Likewise, Christ uttered His complaint of what He had suffered. Physicians tell us that in crucifixion, the whole body is in agony with terrible fever and pain. Our Lord endured it all and cried, "*I thirst.*" He sacrificed both soul and body to the Father.

And now comes the great word: "*It is finished.*" All that there was to suffer and endure had been suffered and endured. He had finished the work the Father gave Him to do. His love held nothing back. He gave Himself as an offering and a sacrifice. Such was the mind of Christ and such must be the attitude of everyone who owes himself and his life to that sacrifice. The mind that was in Christ must be in us, ready to say, "I have come '*to do the will of him that sent me, and to finish his work*'" (John 4:34). And every day that our confidence grows fuller in Christ's finished work, our hearts must more entirely yield themselves as burnt offerings in the service of God and His love.

THE DEATH OF THE CROSS

Father, into thy hands I commend my spirit:
and having said thus, he gave up the ghost.
—Luke 23:46

Like David, Christ had often committed His spirit into the hands of the Father for His daily life and needs. (See Psalm 31:5.) But here is something new and very special. He gave up His spirit into the power of death, gave up all control over it, and sank down into the darkness and death of the grave, where He could neither think, pray, nor will. He surrendered Himself completely into the Father's hands, trusting Him to care for Him in the dark and in due time to raise Him up again.

If we have indeed died in Christ and are now to carry about with us the death of our Lord Jesus in faith every day (see 2 Corinthians 4:10), this word is the one that we need. Just think once again what Christ meant when He said that we must hate and lose our lives. (See John 12:24–25.)

We died in Adam; the life we receive from him is death; there is nothing good or heavenly in us by nature. It is to this inward evil nature, to all the life that we have from this world, that we must die. There cannot be any thought of any real holiness without totally dying to this self, this *"old man"* (Romans 6:6). Many people deceive themselves because they seek to be alive in God before they are dead to their own natures—something as impossible as a grain of wheat being alive before it dies. This total dying to self lies at the root of all true piety. Spiritual life must grow out of death.

And if you ask how you can do this, you will find the answer in the mind in which Christ died. Like Him, you may cast yourself upon God, without knowing how the new life is to be attained. But as you say in fellowship with Jesus, *"Father, into thy hands I commend my spirit,"* and as you depend simply and absolutely on God to raise you up into the new life, the wonderful promise of God's Word will be fulfilled in you. You will know *"what is the exceeding greatness of his power to us-ward who believe, according to the working of his mighty power, which he wrought in Christ, when he raised him from the dead"* (Ephesians 1:19–20).

This is indeed the true rest of faith: living every day and every hour in absolute dependence on the continual and immediate quickening of the divine life in us by God Himself through the Holy Spirit.

— 45 —

IT IS FINISHED

When Jesus therefore had received the vinegar,
he said, It is finished.
—John 19:30

Once again, these words of our Lord on the cross reveal to us His mind and disposition. At the beginning of His ministry when His disciples urged Him to eat, He said, *"My meat is to do the will of him that sent me, and to finish his work"* (John 4:34). In all things, the small as well as the great, He would accomplish God's work. In His high priestly prayer at the end of the three years' ministry, He could say, *"I have glorified thee on the earth: I have finished the work which thou gavest me to do"* (John 17:4). He sacrificed all, and in dying on the cross could in truth say, *"It is finished."*

With these words to the Father, Christ laid down His life. With these words, He was strengthened, after the terrible agony on the cross, in the knowledge that all was now fulfilled. And with these words, He uttered the truth of the gospel of our redemption, that all that was needed for man's salvation had been accomplished on the cross.

This disposition should characterize every follower of Christ. The mind that was in Him must be in us (see Philippians 2:5)—it must be our food, the strength of our lives, to do the will of God in all things and to finish His work. There may be small things about which we are not aware that bring harm to ourselves and to God's work. Or we might draw back before some great thing that demands too much sacrifice. No matter what happens, however, we may find strength to perform our duty in Christ's words: *"It is finished."* His finished work secured the victory over every foe. By faith we may take hold of these dying words of Christ on the cross and may find the power for daily living and daily dying in the fellowship of the crucified Christ.

Child of God, study the inexhaustible treasure contained in this Scripture: *"It is finished."* Faith in what Christ accomplished on the cross will enable you to manifest in daily life the spirit of the cross.

— 46 —

DEAD TO SIN

How shall we, that are dead to sin, live any longer therein?
—Romans 6:2

In the first section of his epistle to the Romans, Paul had expounded the great doctrine of justification by faith. (See Romans 1:16–5:11.) After having done this, Paul proceeded in the second section to unfold the related doctrine of the new life by faith in Christ. (See Romans 5:12–8:39.) Using Adam as an illustration of Christ, Paul taught that, just as we all died in Adam and his death reigns in our natures, so those who believe in Christ actually died to sin in Him, were set free from it, and became partakers of the new holy life of Christ.

Paul asked, *"How shall we, that are dead to sin, live any longer therein?"* In these words, we have the deep spiritual truth that our death to sin in Christ delivers us from its power, so that we no longer can or need to live in it. The secret of true and full holiness is to live, by faith and in the power of the Holy Spirit, with the knowledge that you are dead to sin.

In expounding this truth, Paul reminded the Romans that they were baptized into the death of Christ. *"Therefore we are buried with him by baptism into death....We have been planted together in the likeness of his death....Our old man is crucified with him, that the body of sin might be destroyed"* (Romans 6:4–6). Sin has been rendered void and powerless. Take time to quietly ask for the teaching of the Holy Spirit. Ponder these words until this truth masters you: you are indeed dead to sin in Christ Jesus. As you grow in the consciousness of your union with the crucified Christ, you will experience that the power of His life in you has made you free from the power of sin.

Romans 6 is one of the most blessed portions of the New Testament of our Lord Jesus, teaching us that our *"old man,"* the old nature that is in us, was actually crucified with Him, so that we no longer need to be in bondage to sin. But remember, only as the Holy Spirit makes Christ's death a reality within us will we know—not by force of argument or conviction, but in the reality of the power of a divine life—that we are indeed dead to sin. It only requires the continual living in Christ Jesus.

DEAD WITH CHRIST

Now if we be dead with Christ,
we believe that we shall also live with him.
—Romans 6:8

The reason God's children live so little in the power of the resurrection life of Christ is that they have so little understanding of, or faith in, their death with Christ. How clearly this appears from what Paul said: *"Now if we be dead with Christ, we believe that we shall also live with him."* Such is the knowledge and experience that give us the assurance of His resurrection power in us. *"He died unto sin once: but in that he liveth, he liveth unto God"* (verse 10). Only as we know that we are dead with Him can we live with Him.

On the strength of this, Paul pleaded earnestly with his readers: *"Likewise reckon ye also yourselves to be dead indeed unto sin, but alive unto God through Jesus Christ our Lord"* (verse 11). The words *"likewise reckon ye also yourselves"* are a call to bold, confident faith. *"Reckon ye also yourselves to be dead indeed unto sin"* as much as Christ is, *"but alive unto God through Jesus Christ."* These words give us a divine assurance of what we actually are and have in Christ—not as a truth that our minds can master and take hold of, but as a reality that the Holy Spirit will reveal within us. In His power, we accept our death with Christ on the cross as the power of our daily lives.

Then we are able to accept and obey the command: *"Let not sin therefore reign in your mortal body...but yield yourselves unto God, as those that are alive from the dead....For sin shall not have dominion* over you" (verses 12–14). *"Being then made free from sin, ye became the servants of righteousness....So now yield your members servants to righteousness unto holiness....But now being made free from sin...ye have your fruit unto holiness"* (verses 18–19, 22).

All of Romans 6 is a wonderful revelation of the deep meaning of its opening words: *"How shall we, that are dead to sin, live any longer therein?"* (verse 2). Everything depends on our acceptance of the divine assurance that if we died with Christ, we have the power to live for God, just as Christ who died now lives for God.

— 48 —

DEAD TO THE LAW

*Ye also are become dead to the law by the body of Christ....that
being dead wherein we were held;
that we should serve in newness of spirit.*
—Romans 7:4, 6

The believer is not only dead to sin, but also dead to the law. This is a deeper truth, giving us deliverance from the thought of a life of effort and failure, and opening the way to life in the power of the Holy Spirit. *"Thou shalt"* is done away with; the power of the Spirit takes its place.

In the remainder of Romans 7, we find a description of the Christian as he still tries to obey the law but utterly fails. His experience is such that he says, *"In me (that is, in my flesh,) dwelleth no good thing"* (verse 18). He discovers that the law of sin, notwithstanding his greatest efforts, continually brings him into captivity and causes him to cry out, *"O wretched man that I am! who shall deliver me from the body of this death?"* (verse 24). In the whole passage, "I" is everywhere, without any thought of the Spirit's help. Only when he has cried out in despair is he brought to see that he is no longer under the law, but under the rule of the Holy Spirit. *"There is therefore now no condemnation"*—such as he had experienced in his attempt to obey the law—*"to them which are in Christ Jesus....For the law of the Spirit of life in Christ Jesus hath made me free from the law of sin and death"* (Romans 8:1–2).

As Romans 7 gives us the experience that leads to being a captive under the power of sin, chapter 8 reveals the experience of a man in

Christ Jesus who has now been made free from the law of sin and death. In the former, we have the life of the ordinary Christian doing his utmost to keep the commandments of the law and walk in God's ways, but always ending in failure and shortcoming. In the latter, we have the man who knows that he is in Christ Jesus, dead to sin and alive to God, and by the Spirit has been made free and is kept free from the bondage of sin and death.

Oh, that men understood the deep meaning of Romans 7, where a man learns that in him, in his flesh, there is no good thing, and no deliverance from this condition except by yielding to the power of the Spirit! Only in this way can men be free from the bondage of the flesh and can fulfill the righteousness of the law in the power of Christ.

THE FLESH CONDEMNED ON THE CROSS

For what the law could not do, in that it was weak through the flesh, God sending his own Son in the likeness of sinful flesh, and for sin, condemned sin in the flesh.
—Romans 8:3

In Romans 8:7, Paul wrote, *"The carnal mind"*—that is, the mind of the flesh—*"is enmity against God: for it is not subject to the law of God, neither indeed can be."* Here Paul opened up the depth of sin that is in the flesh. In chapter 7, he said in his flesh *"dwelleth no good thing"* (verse 18). Here he went deeper and told us that the flesh is *"enmity against God"*; it hates God and His law. It was on this account that God condemned sin in the flesh on the cross; all the curse that is on sin is on the flesh in which sin dwells. As the believer understands this, he will cease from any attempt at seeking to perfect in the flesh what is begun in the Spirit. (See Galatians 3:3.) The two are at deadly, irreconcilable enmity.

This lies at the very root of the true Christian life:

God sending his own Son in the likeness of sinful flesh, and for sin, condemned sin in the flesh: that the righteousness of the law might be fulfilled in us, who walk not after the flesh, but after the Spirit. (Romans 8:3–4)

All the requirements of God's law will be fulfilled not in those who strive to keep and fulfill that law—thing that is utterly impossible—but in those who walk by the Spirit and, in His power, live out the life that Christ won for us on the cross and imparted to us in the resurrection.

May God's children learn the double lesson here. In our flesh, in the old nature we have from Adam, there dwells literally no good thing that can satisfy the eye of a holy God. And that flesh can never by any process of discipline, struggling, or prayer be made better than it is. But the Son of God, in the likeness of sinful flesh and in the form of a man, condemned sin on the cross.

> *There is therefore now no condemnation to them which are in Christ Jesus, who walk not after the flesh, but after the Spirit.* (Romans 8:1)

— 50 —

JESUS CHRIST
AND HIM CRUCIFIED

*For I determined not to know any thing among you, save Jesus
Christ, and him crucified....And my speech and my preaching
was...in demonstration of the Spirit and of power.*
—1 Corinthians 2:2, 4

This passage of Scripture is very often understood to mean that
Paul's purpose in his preaching was to know nothing but Jesus Christ
and Him crucified. But it contains a far deeper meaning. Paul spoke
of his purpose, not only in the matter of his preaching, but also in his
whole spirit and life, in order to prove how he in everything sought to
act in conformity to the crucified Christ. Thus he wrote that Christ
*"was crucified through weakness, yet he liveth by the power of God. For
we also are weak in him, but we shall live with him by the power of God
toward you"* (2 Corinthians 13:4).

Paul's whole ministry and all his actions bore the mark of Christ's
likeness; he was crucified through weakness, yet he lived by the power
of God. Just before the words of our text, Paul had written, *"For the
preaching of the cross is to them that perish foolishness; but unto us which
are saved it is the power of God"* (1 Corinthians 1:18). Not only in his
preaching, but also in all his activities and behavior, he sought to act
in harmony with the weakness in which Christ was crucified. He had
so identified himself with the weakness of the cross and its shame
that, in his whole life and conduct, he proved that he sought to show
forth the likeness and the spirit of the crucified Jesus in everything.

Hence he said, *"And I was with you in weakness, and in fear, and in much trembling"* (1 Corinthians 2:3).

It is on this account that he spoke so strongly and said, *"Christ sent me…to preach the gospel: not with wisdom of words, lest the cross of Christ should be made of none effect"* (1 Corinthians 1:17). *"And my speech and my preaching was not with enticing words of man's wisdom, but in demonstration of the Spirit and of power"* (1 Corinthians 2:4). Is this not the great reason why the power of God is so little manifested in the preaching of the gospel? Christ the Crucified One may be the subject of the preaching, and yet, because of men's confidence in human learning and eloquence, there may be none of the likeness of the crucified Jesus that alone gives preaching its supernatural, divine power.

God help us to understand how the life of every minister and every believer must bear the stamp of the sanctuary—nothing but Jesus Christ and Him crucified.

51

TEMPERATE IN ALL THINGS

Every man that striveth for the mastery is temperate in all things....I keep under my body, and bring it into subjection.
—1 Corinthians 9:25, 27

Here Paul reminded us of the wellknown principle that anyone competing for a prize is *"temperate in all things."* Everything, however attractive, that might be a hindrance in the race is given up or set aside. And this is done in order to obtain an earthly prize. We who strive for an incorruptible crown (verse 25) and strive so that Christ may be Lord of all—will we not be *"temperate in all things"* that could in the very least prevent our following the Lord Jesus with an undivided heart?

Paul said, *"I keep under my body, and bring it into subjection."* He would allow nothing to hinder him. He told us, *"One thing I do...I press toward the mark for the prize of the high calling of God in Christ Jesus"* (Philippians 3:13–14). No self-pleasing in eating and drinking, no comfort or ease, would for a moment have kept him from showing the spirit of the cross in his daily life, or from sacrificing all, like his Master. Read the following four passages that comprise Paul's life history: 1 Corinthians 4:11–13; 2 Corinthians 4:8–12; 2 Corinthians 6:4–10; and 2 Corinthians 11:23–27. The cross was not only the theme of his preaching, but also the rule of his life in all its details.

We need to ask God that this disposition may be found in all Christians and preachers of the gospel, through the power of the Holy

Spirit. When the death of Christ works with power in the preacher, then Christ's life will be known among the people. Let us pray that the fellowship of the cross may regain its old place, and that God's children may obey the command: *"Let this mind be in you, which was also in Christ Jesus"* (Philippians 2:5). *"He humbled himself, and became obedient unto death, even the death of the cross"* (verse 8).

> *For if we have been planted together in the likeness of his death, we shall be also in the likeness of his resurrection.*
>
> (Romans 6:5)

52

THE DYING OF THE LORD JESUS

Always bearing about in the body the dying of the Lord Jesus,
that the life also of Jesus might be made manifest in our body....
So then death worketh in us, but life in you.
—2 Corinthians 4:10, 12

Paul was very bold in speaking of the intimate union that was between the life of Christ in him and the life he lived in the flesh with all its suffering. In Galatians 2:20, he had spoken of being crucified with Christ and of Christ living in him. Here he talked about how he was *"bearing about in the body the dying of the Lord Jesus"*; it was through this that the life of Jesus was also manifested in his body. And he told the Corinthians that because the death of Christ was thus working in and through him, Christ's life could work in them.

We often speak of abiding in Christ, but we forget that this means abiding in a crucified Christ. Many believers seem to think that once they have claimed Christ's death in the fellowship of the cross and have considered themselves as crucified with Him, they may now consider it as over and done with. They do not understand that it is in the crucified Christ, and in the fellowship of His death, that they are to abide daily and unceasingly. The fellowship of the cross is to be a daily experience. The self-emptying of our Lord, His taking the form of a servant, His humbling Himself and becoming *"obedient unto death, even the death of the cross"* (Philippians 2:8)—this mind that was in Christ is to be the disposition that marks our daily lives.

"Always bearing about in the body the dying of the Lord Jesus"—this is what we are called to as much as Paul was. If we are indeed to live for the welfare of others around us, if we are to sacrifice our ease and pleasure to win souls for our Lord, it will be true of us as of Paul, that we are able to say, *"Death worketh in us, but life in"* those for whom we pray and labor. It is in *"the fellowship of his sufferings"* (Philippians 3:10) that the crucified Lord can live and work out His life in us and through us.

Let us learn the lesson that the abiding in Christ Jesus, for which we have so often prayed and worked, is nothing less than the abiding of the crucified Lord in us, and we in Him.

— 53 —

THE CROSS AND THE SPIRIT

How much more shall the blood of Christ, who through the
eternal Spirit offered himself without blemish unto God, cleanse
your conscience?
—Hebrews 9:14 RV

The cross is Christ's highest glory. The glory that He received from the Father was entirely owing to His having humbled Himself to the death of the cross. *"Wherefore God also hath highly exalted him"* (Philippians 2:9). The greatest work that the Holy Spirit could ever do in the Son of God was when He enabled Him to yield Himself as a sacrifice and an offering for a sweet smelling savor. And the Holy Spirit can now do nothing greater or more glorious for us than to lead us into the fellowship and likeness of that crucified life of our Lord.

Do we not have here the reason that our prayers for the mighty working of the Holy Spirit are not more abundantly answered? We have prayed too little that the Holy Spirit might glorify Christ in us in the fellowship of and the conformity to His sufferings. (See Philippians 3:10.) The Spirit who led Christ to the cross desires and is able to maintain in us the life of abiding in the crucified Jesus.

The Spirit and the cross are inseparable. The Spirit led Christ to the cross; the cross brought Christ to the throne to receive the fullness of the Spirit to impart to His people. The Spirit taught Peter to preach Christ crucified; it was through this preaching that the three thousand received the Spirit. (See Acts 2:14–41.) In the preaching of the gospel, in the Christian life, the Spirit and the cross are inseparable; as it was in Christ, so it must be in us. The sad lack of the mind and disposition of the crucified Christ—sacrificing self and the world to win life for the dying—is one great cause of the feebleness of the church. Let us ask God fervently to teach us to say, "We have been crucified with Christ; in Him we have died to sin." Let us always carry *about in the body the dying of the Lord Jesus* (2 Corinthians 4:10). In this way we will be prepared for the fullness of the Spirit that the Father desires to bestow.

— 54 —

THE VEIL OF THE FLESH

*Having therefore, brethren, boldness to enter into the holiest by
the blood of Jesus, by a new and living way, which he hath con-
secrated for us, through the veil, that is to say, his flesh.*
—Hebrews 10:19–20

In the temple, there was a veil between the holy place and the holiest of all. At the altar in the court, the blood of the sacrifice was sprin-
kled for forgiveness of sins. This gave the priest entrance into the holy
place to offer incense to God as part of a holy worship. But into the
holiest of all, behind the veil, the high priest alone might enter once
a year. This veil was the symbol of sinful human nature; even though
it had received the forgiveness of sin, full access and fellowship with
God was impossible.

When Christ died, the veil was torn in two. Christ dedicated *"a
new and living way"* to God through the torn veil of His flesh. This
new way, by which we now can enter into the holiest of all, always
passes through the torn veil of the flesh. Every believer has *"crucified
the flesh with the affections and lusts"* (Galatians 5:24). Every step on
the *"new and living way"* for entering into God's holy presence maintains the fellowship with the cross of Christ. The torn veil of the flesh
refers not only to Christ and His sufferings, but also to our experience in the likeness of His sufferings.

Is this not the reason why many Christians can never attain close
fellowship with God? They have never yielded the flesh as an accursed
thing to the condemnation of the cross. They desire to enter into the

holiest of all, yet they allow *"the flesh with the affections and lusts"* to rule over them. God grant that we may rightly understand, in the power of the Holy Spirit, that Christ has called us to hate our lives, to lose our lives, and to be dead with Him to sin so that we may live to God with Him.

There is no way to a full, abiding fellowship with God except through the torn veil of the flesh, through a life with the flesh crucified in Christ Jesus. God be praised that the Holy Spirit always dwells in us to keep the flesh in its place of crucifixion and condemnation, and to give us the abiding victory over all temptations.

55

LOOKING TO JESUS

Let us run with patience the race that is set before us,
looking unto Jesus the author and perfecter of our faith,
who for the joy that was set before him endured
the cross, despising shame.
—Hebrews 12:1–2 RV

In running a race, a person's eyes and heart are always set upon the goal and the prize. In Hebrews 12, the Christian is called to keep his eyes focused on Jesus, who endured the cross, as the one object of imitation and desire. In our whole lives, we are always to be animated by His Spirit as He bore the cross. This was the way that led to the throne and the glory of God. This is the *"new and living way"* (Hebrews 10:20) that He opened for us through the veil of the flesh. As we study and realize that God so highly exalted His Son because He bore the cross (see Philippians 2:9), we will walk in His footsteps, bearing our own crosses as He did, with our flesh condemned and crucified.

The powerlessness of the church is greatly owing to the fact that this crossbearing mind of Jesus is so little preached and practiced. Most Christians think that as long as they do not commit obvious sins, they are at liberty to possess and enjoy as much of the world as they please. There is so little insight into the deep truth that the world, and the flesh that loves the world, is *"enmity against God"* (Romans 8:7). Hence, many Christians seek and pray for conformity to the image of Jesus for years and fail so entirely. They do not know, they do not seek with the whole heart to know, what it is to die to self and the world.

It was "*for the joy that was set before him,*" the joy of pleasing and glorifying the Father, the joy of loving and winning souls for Himself, that Christ endured the cross. We have a great need for a new crusade with the proclamation, "This is the will of God: just as Christ, through His endurance of the cross, found His highest happiness and received from the Father the fullness of the Spirit to pour down on His people, so it is only in our fellowship of the cross that we can really become '*conformed to the image of his Son*' (Romans 8:29)." As believers awake to this blessed truth, and as they always look to the crucified Jesus while running the race, they will receive power to win for Christ the souls He purchased on the cross.

56

ALIVE UNTO RIGHTEOUSNESS

Who his own self bare our sins in his body upon the tree,
that we, having died unto sins, might live unto righteousness.
—1 Peter 2:24 RV

Here in the epistle of Peter we have the same lessons that Paul taught us. First is the atonement of the cross: *"Who his own self bare our sins in his body upon the tree."* And then comes the fellowship of the cross: *"That we, having died unto sins, might live unto righteousness."*

In this last expression, we have the great thought that a Christian cannot live to righteousness unless he knows that he has died to sin. We need the Holy Spirit to make our death to sin such a reality that we know we are forever free from its power and will therefore yield our whole selves *"as instruments of righteousness unto God"* (Romans 6:13).

Dear Christian, it cost Christ much to bear the cross and then to yield Himself so that it could bear Him. It cost Him much when He cried, *"Now is my soul troubled; and what shall I say? Father, save me from this hour: but for this cause came I unto this hour"* (John 12:27).

Let us not imagine that the fellowship of the cross—concerning which Peter wrote the words, *"That we, having died unto sins, might live unto righteousness"*—is easily understood or experienced. It means that the Holy Spirit will teach us what it is to be identified with Christ in His cross. It means that we realize by faith how we truly shared with Christ in His death, and now, as He lives in us, we abide in unceasing fellowship with Him, the Crucified One. This requires self-sacrifice, earnest prayer, and a wholehearted surrender to God, His will, and the cross of Jesus. It requires abiding in Christ and having unceasing fellowship with Him.

A PRAYER

Blessed Lord, reveal to us each day through the Holy Spirit the secret of our lives in You—we in You, and You in us. Let Your Spirit reveal to us that as truly as we died in You, You now live in us the life that was crucified and now is glorified in heaven. Let Your Spirit burn the words deep into our hearts. Having died to sin, and being forever set free from its dominion, let us know that sin can no more reign over us or have dominion. In the power of Your redemption, let us yield ourselves to You as those who are alive from the dead, ready and prepared for all Your will. Amen.

57

FOLLOWERS OF THE CROSS

Hereby perceive we the love of God,
because he laid down his life for us:
and we ought to lay down our lives for the brethren.
—1 John 3:16

Greater love hath no man than this, that a man lay down his life for *his friends*" (John 15:13). Here our Lord revealed to us the inconceivable love that moved Him to die for us. And now, under the influence and in the power of that love dwelling in us, comes the message: "*We ought to lay down our lives for the brethren.*" Nothing less is expected of us than a Christlike life and a Christlike love, proving itself in all our fellowship with our fellow believers.

The cross of Christ is the measure by which we know how much Christ loves us. That cross is also the measure of the love that we owe to the believers around us. Only as the love of Christ on the cross possesses our hearts and daily animates our whole beings will we be able to love others. Our fellowship in the cross of Christ is to manifest itself in our sacrifice of love, not only to Christ Himself, but also to all who belong to Him.

The life to which John here called us is something entirely supernatural and divine. Only the faith of Christ Himself living in us can enable us to accept this great command in the assurance that Christ Himself will work it out in us. It is He Himself who calls us: "*If any man will come after me, let him deny himself, and take up his cross, and follow me*" (Matthew 16:24). Nothing less than this—a dying to our own natures, a faith that our *"old man"* (Romans 6:6), our flesh, has been crucified with Christ, so that we no longer need to sin—can enable us to say, "We love His commandments; this commandment, too, is not grievous." (See 1 John 5:3.)

But for such fellowship and conformity to the death of Christ, nothing will be effective except the daily, unbroken abiding in Christ Jesus that He has promised us. By the Holy Spirit revealing and glorifying Christ in us, we may trust Christ Himself to live out His life in us. He who proved His love on the cross of Calvary, He alone can enable us to say in truth, *"He laid down his life for us: and we ought to lay down our lives for the brethren."* Only as the great truth of the indwelling Christ obtains a place in the faith of the church that it does not have now, will the Christlike love for other believers become the mark of true Christianity, by which all men will know that we are Christ's disciples. (See John 13:35.) This is what will bring the world to believe that God has loved us even as He loved Christ. (See John 17:23.)

58

FOLLOWING THE LAMB

These are they which follow the Lamb
whithersoever he goeth.
—Revelation 14:4

It may not be easy to say exactly what is implied in this following of the Lamb in the heavenly vision. But of this we may be sure: it will be the counterpart in heaven of what it is to follow in the footsteps of the Lamb here upon earth. As the Lamb on earth revealed what the Lamb in heaven would be, so His followers on earth can show forth something of the glory of what it will be to follow Him in heaven.

And how may the footsteps of the Lamb be known? *"He humbled himself"* (Philippians 2:8). *"As a lamb to the slaughter…he opened not his mouth"* (Isaiah 53:7). The meekness, gentleness, and humility that marked Him are the very things that call His followers to walk in His footsteps.

Our Lord Himself said, *"Learn of me; for I am meek and lowly in heart: and ye shall find rest unto your souls"* (Matthew 11:29). Paul wrote:

> *Let this mind be in you, which was also in Christ Jesus: who, being in the form of God, thought it not robbery to be equal with God: but made himself of no reputation, and took upon him the form of a servant, and was made in the likeness of men: and being found in fashion as a man, he humbled himself, and became obedient unto death, even the death of the cross.*
> (Philippians 2:5–8)

The Lamb is our Lord and Lawgiver. He opened the only path that leads to the throne of God. As we learn from Him what it means to be meek and lowly, what it means to empty ourselves, to choose the place of the servant, to humble ourselves and become obedient, even to the death of the cross, we will find the *"new and living way"* (Hebrews 10:20) that leads us through the torn veil into the holiest of all.

"Wherefore God also hath highly exalted him, and given him a name which is above every name" (Philippians 2:9). Because Christians so little bear the mark of this self-emptying and humiliation even unto death, the world refuses to believe in the possibility of a Christfilled life.

O child of God, come and study the Lamb who is to be your model and your Savior. Let Paul's words be the keynote of your life: *"I am crucified with Christ: nevertheless I live; yet not I, but Christ liveth in me"* (Galatians 2:20). This is the way to follow the Lamb even to the glory of the throne of God in heaven.

59

TO HIM BE THE GLORY

Unto him that loved us, and washed us from our sins
in his own blood, and hath made us kings and priests unto God
and his Father; to him be glory and dominion
for ever and ever. Amen.
—Revelation 1:5–6

Some of my readers may feel that it is not easy to understand the lesson of the cross or carry it out in their lives. Do not think of it as a heavy burden or yoke that you have to bear. Christ has said, *"My yoke is easy, and my burden is light"* (Matthew 11:30). Love makes everything easy. Do not think of *your* love for Him, but of *His* great love for you, given through the Holy Spirit. Meditate on this day and night, until you have the assurance that He loves you unspeakably. It is through the love of Christ on the cross that souls are drawn to Him.

We have here the answer for what will enable us to love the fellowship of the crucified Jesus. It is nothing less than His love poured out through the continual inspiration of the Holy Spirit into the heart of every child of God.

"Unto him that loved us." Be still, dear soul, and think what this everlasting love is that seeks to take possession of you and fill you with unspeakable joy.

"And washed us from our sins in his own blood." Is this not proof enough that He will never reject you, that you are precious in His sight, and that through the power of His blood you are well pleasing to God?

"And hath made us kings and priests unto God and his Father." He now preserves us by His power. He will strengthen us through His Spirit to reign as kings over sin and the world, to appear as priests before God in intercession for others. O Christian, learn this wonderful song, and repeat it until your heart is filled with love, joy, and courage, and it turns to Him in glad surrender every day. *"To him be glory and dominion for ever and ever. Amen."*

Yes, to Him, who has loved me, has washed me from my sins in His blood, and has made me a king and a priest—to Him be the glory in all ages. Amen.

60

THE BLESSING OF THE CROSS

But God forbid that I should glory,
save in the cross of our Lord Jesus Christ, by whom the
world is crucified unto me, and I unto the world.
—Galatians 6:14

One of the blessings of the cross consists in this: it teaches us to know the worthlessness of our efforts and the utter corruption of our own natures. The cross does not offer to improve human nature or supply what man is unable to do. Indeed, many people use it in this way, like patching a new cloth on an old garment. But this tears the garment, and such people walk around in torn clothes, going from one minister to another, without finding what they seek. No, the old garment, our *"old man"* (Romans 6:6), must be laid aside and given over to the death of the cross. And the cross causes all that is of the lost nature of man to die the accursed death, and the "I" takes the place of an evildoer; all that is of the old nature is broken by the cross.

Whoever has been brought to the cross through the Spirit has learned to pronounce the death sentence on his old nature; he has broken the staff over himself, for whatever does not bear the mark of the cross lies under the curse. He who wishes to save his life remains under the curse. If we have learned through the Spirit to understand the cross, then we have lost our lives. We will no longer expect any good from our old natures, and will not judge others, but only ourselves.

But as long as we have not been taught this lesson through the Spirit, we will try to find good in ourselves, something of worth in God's sight, upon which the sentence of death need not be passed. And if we find nothing at all, we fall into a false grief, which the evil one eagerly uses to make us despair by saying, "You may as well give up; God will not bother with you; there is nothing for you but failure."

This is not what God desires, however. What we possess by nature must be nailed to the cross, and we must put on the new man. The cross brings us to utter bankruptcy of ourselves, and then God can come to our aid. The cross brought the disciples of Jesus to an end of themselves; even the words of the Master had failed to do this. It took from them the halo of holiness they thought they had won in the three years they followed Jesus, and it taught them to know themselves. And so they were prepared to receive the Holy Spirit, who would impart a new nature and a new life to them. For we cannot separate the cross from the Spirit. We can have no Easter and no Pentecost until we have first had a Good Friday.

Through the cross alone are we prepared for life in the fullness of God; only he who is crucified with Christ can become a *"vessel unto honour"* (2 Timothy 2:21).

Our *"old man"* (Romans 6:6) must be crucified with Christ. In the resurrection of Christ we find the roots of our new life. (See 1 Peter 1:3). Whoever loses his life will find it. (See Matthew 10:39.) We must learn the lesson of the cross, as condemned and rejected ones who have been crucified with Christ. Then the door will be open for a life of power and blessing. All that belongs to death must be given over to death, even as the body is buried in the earth because it belongs to the earth.

The Holy Spirit, the eternal Spirit, is unchangeable. He brought Christ our Head to the cross, and us His children with Him. This work in us is twofold. On the one hand, it leads us to death and all that belongs to death; and on the other hand, it leads us to the life that God has placed within us, leading from glory to glory.

— SECTION THREE —

THE SECRET OF
THE ABIDING PRESENCE

I n *The International Review of Missions*, the editor wrote and printed an article on "The Missionary and His Task."[2] He told of a pamphlet that had been issued to a large number of missionaries, inviting them to state the problems that, within the past year or two, had chiefly claimed their attention. In answer, 233 replies had been received from missionaries belonging to fifty different missionary societies. The editor thought that these responses were a sample of missionary thought that could seriously represent what missionaries as a whole were thinking.

After a short survey of the chief problems to which the missionaries referred, the article tells us that the most difficult problems were those dealing with the personal life of the missionary, according to many of the correspondents. A few quotations from their letters, showing their needs and desires, follow.

"One of the most pressing problems of late years has been the possibility of getting one person to do three people's work. And the question to be faced is how to live so that the things of heaven will not be crowded out by the things of earth. One's duties are so multitudinous that it is often impossible to make those opportunities for personal contact which are so important," wrote one of the respondents.

A missionary of more than ordinary ability, who had seen twenty years of service in India, wrote, "The problem is the personal one. I am the greatest problem I have to deal with in my work. Spiritually, I am always ready to be offered, but missionary work means more than

2. *The International Review of Missions*, Vol. 3, edited by J. H. Oldham (London: Oxford University Press, April 1914), 284-296.

this. It means adequate and real effectiveness as a source of spiritual inspiration to my work, to my people, to my brethren. What we need to face is the problem of how to make and keep the average missionary a more spiritual man, a bigger and more constant spiritual force in what the man himself is."

Another writer referred to the temptation to secularity that is always present in missionary work: "How to do the day's work and get sufficient sleep, and also get the time for Bible study and prayer that is essential—these are often the hardest battles that the missionary has to fight."

A leading missionary wrote, "The most pressing problem here, as at home, would seem to be the difficulty of avoiding such overactivity as saps the springs of spiritual life in missionaries themselves—of perseverance in following the hidden, childlike life of our Lord, and so manifesting His life to the people around."

Another experienced missionary wrote, "Within the mission field, the greatest problem would seem to be that of securing real Christian love and unity among the workers themselves, foreigners and Indians together, 'that the world may know that thou hast sent me' (John 17:23). Supernatural power alone can bring this about."

Another correspondent said, "There is only one problem, and that is faith. We do not believe that God is in control, and so there are infinite problems, as we try to run the church or the work ourselves. Yet they are really not problems of ours at all, but His problems."

It is difficult to express what I felt as I read this article more than once and wondered what was to be done to meet this need of God's dear children, men and women who have not considered their lives dear to themselves, but have sacrificed all to bring His blessed gospel to the unsaved.

One missionary felt that the first thing to be done was to pray. And yet, what to pray? Where to begin and what to expect? Would our prayers reach these men and women? We might just put the 233 correspondents on our prayer list and ask God to guide us and show us what we ought to think, what to desire, and what to hope for.

Then the thought came to me that these 233 are only the evidence of how many of the multitudes of missionaries scattered throughout the world may also share the difficulties and the burdens I have mentioned, and may deeply need to know the secret of being kept and guided in the light and the joy of abiding communion with their blessed Lord. Prayer came more fervently than ever, and then I had the further thought: it is not in the missionaries, but in the home church that has sent them, that the root of the trouble is to be found. The church does not live in that full experience of the knowledge of Jesus as its life and strength that would sustain its messengers to the unsaved and would keep them, in the midst of all their trials, in perfect peace.

The closing words in the article give us in one sentence what the real lack is and what is the only way of deliverance: "I believe that when we see with real intensity of vision what the life of faith is, and as a consequence feel with real intensity how full of unbelief our lives are, both as a church and as individuals, and frankly confess it as a practical matter, then life will be aglow with the presence of God."

But it is exactly the vision of the life of faith that is so little known. When that is really given, when we begin to be ashamed of our unbelief, and when we frankly confess that we have been living lives of unbelief in not fully accepting what Christ is willing to be to us, deliverance is drawing near.

On His last night, our Lord spoke distinctly about the life of the Father in Him here on earth being the very life that He would live in His disciples: *"I in them, and thou in me"* (John 17:23). This is the life of faith: to believe not only that Christ has died for us, pardoned us, and made us God's children, but also that He lives in us and keeps us in abiding and unbroken fellowship with Himself. When a child of God sees that this is what Christ has promised and sees what He is able by His almighty power to perform and make real in us, he will be prepared to understand how his life every hour of the day can be in the power of Christ's keeping and guidance. However difficult it may appear to act this faith and commit oneself in the surrender of an absolute helplessness to this almighty Christ, *they shall not be ashamed that wait for*" the Lord (Isaiah 49:23).

Later on, another article appeared in *The International Review of Missions* entitled "The Devotional Life of the Missionary,"[3] in which many of the same ideas were expressed as in the prior article. The writer, Miss A. H. Small, was a missionary in India for sixteen years and principal of a women's missionary college in Edinburgh for ten years. She wrote of having a large and intimate correspondence with missionaries of the younger generation in almost every mission field—a correspondence that she felt gave her a very fair indication of the minds and desires of younger missionaries at any given time.

She wrote, "There is one subject that recurs constantly and with great urgency of feeling. It is a matter for serious consideration and deeply concerns the whole of life, relationship, and service. It is the subject of the devotional life. How to secure time for the quiet hour with God in an overcrowded day, and how best to use it when secured, are the anxious considerations of a large number of men and women in every field. Indeed, many frankly state that their own feebleness as missionaries and the comparative inadequacy of missionary results in proportion to missionary endeavors, are almost entirely caused by their failure, both individually and collectively, to make the time for daily communion with God and to rightly use that time....A few quotations from letters will illustrate what is meant.

'I would need to have time to pray until love burns away the sloth and the weariness and the sin.'

'Our greatest need is to resist the temptation to do more than we can do in the right spirit; and to crush out with actual work the time that should be spent in waiting upon God in quietness.'

---

3. *The International Review of Missions*, Vol. 3, July 1914, 447-455.

'The want of quiet [with God] is at the root of all my failure; and the struggle to get it is sometimes desperate.'

'Since I have been able to think about the future of the work here, I am acutely alive to the fact that it is not costing me enough spiritually. It must, even if some of the work has to go.'

'I am afraid of losing sight of the vision while teaching English, arithmetic, and geography at the same hours every day, week after week. Is it not hard to shake oneself up, and to look out for the glory and the gleam in each lesson? I have no doubt it is there, if only I had eyes to see.'

"...No man or woman, at home or abroad, who knows anything at all of the present missionary situation will question that if this problem exists, the solution of it must lie heavily upon the conscience of the whole church....If prayer in these conditions, or in any conditions, is to be anything, it must be everything. If the purpose of God is to be in the missionary movement He must move in the heart of it....If the missionary is rightly to represent and to introduce Jesus Christ our Lord as the Savior into all holy living...he must be so possessed of Him that there can be no mistake regarding the truth of his Gospel....

"If time and place be made in the daily routine—even [though] it may seem at grave expense to work or needful rest—for quiet, unhasting, uninterrupted communion with God, the immediate reward will be twofold: problems of overwork will solve themselves in His presence; and the quiet hour will itself become a constant source of renewal of strength and courage and love. It was a very busy missionary who was wont to say, 'Our Master never asks of us so heavy labour as shall leave us no leisure for sitting at His feet.'"

After I read the article, the question came to me: Does not the root of the difficulty lie in the failure of the church as a whole to enter into the abundance of the life that is in Christ, and to teach the fullness of His power to redeem and to save? Must not the church stand behind its missionaries with a more triumphant gospel if the dead weight of dullness, unspirituality, unbelief, and heathen tradition is to be lifted from the church in the mission field? The tides would surely run more strongly if the church as a whole had a firmer and clearer faith in God, who, as revealed in the New Testament, is overflowing and alive. Here in this personal challenge, we seem to probe the real depths of the problem of the church in the mission field.

A PRAYER

How will I praise You, O my God, for the gift of the Holy Spirit, who will reveal to me the secret of the cross of Christ? The Spirit strengthened Christ to offer Himself to God on the cross. The cross gave Christ the right to receive the fullness of the Spirit from the Father to pour out on all flesh. The cross gives us the right to receive the Spirit. And the Spirit teaches us to love the cross and to partake of the life crucified with Christ.

O my Father, I thank You that You give the direct continual working of the Spirit in my heart, that the crucified Christ may be formed within me, and His life maintained within me. Father, I ask You humbly, teach me and Your people so to know this work of the Spirit and yield ourselves to Him to take full possession of us, that the crucified Lord Jesus may be glorified in us. Amen.

THE ABIDING PRESENCE

Lo, I am with you always, even unto the end of the world.
—Matthew 28:20

When the Lord chose His twelve apostles, it was so *"that they should be with him, and that he might send them forth to preach"* (Mark 3:14). A life in fellowship with Him was to be their preparation for the work of preaching.

The disciples were so deeply conscious of having this great privilege that when Christ spoke of His leaving them to go to the Father, their hearts were filled with great sorrow. The presence of Christ had become indispensable to them; they could not think of living without Him. To comfort them, Christ gave them the promise of the Holy Spirit, with the assurance that they then would have Himself in His heavenly presence in a far deeper and more intimate sense than they ever had known on earth. Their first calling remained unchanged; to be with Him, to live in unbroken fellowship with Him, would be the secret of power to preach and testify of Him.

When Christ gave them the Great Commission to *"go ye therefore, and teach all nations, baptizing them in the name of the Father, and of the Son, and of the Holy Ghost: teaching them to observe all things whatsoever I have commanded you"* (Matthew 28:19–20), He added, *"Lo, I am with you always, even unto the end of the world."*

This principle holds good for all Christ's servants for all time, as it did for the twelve apostles: without the experience of His presence always abiding with them, their preaching would have no power. The secret of their strength would be the living testimony that Jesus Christ was with them every moment, inspiring, directing, and strengthening them. It was this reality that made them so bold in preaching Him as the Crucified One in the midst of His enemies. They never for a moment regretted His bodily absence; they had Him with them and in them, in the divine power of the Holy Spirit.

In all the work of the minister and the missionary, everything depends on an awareness, through a living faith, of the abiding presence of the Lord with His servant. The living experience of the presence of Jesus is an essential element in preaching the gospel. If this is clouded, our work becomes a human effort, without the freshness and the power of the heavenly life. And nothing can bring back the power and the blessing besides a return to the Master's feet, so that He may breathe into the heart, in divine power, His blessed words: *"Lo, I am with you always."*

— 62 —

THE OMNIPOTENCE
OF CHRIST

All power is given unto me in heaven and in earth.
—Matthew 28:18

Before Christ gave His disciples their Great Commission to begin the great world conquest that aimed to bring His gospel to every creature, He first revealed Himself in His divine power as a partner with God Himself, the Almighty. It was their faith in this that enabled the disciples to undertake the work in all simplicity and boldness. They had begun to know Him in the mighty resurrection power that had conquered sin and death; there was nothing too great for Him to command or for them to undertake.

Every disciple of Jesus Christ who desires to take part in *"the victory that overcometh the world"* (1 John 5:4) needs time, faith, and the Holy Spirit. These things are needed so that he may come under the full conviction that he is to take his part in the work as a servant of the omnipotent Lord Jesus. He is to depend on the daily experience of being *"strong in the Lord, and in the power of his might"* (Ephesians 6:10). God's promises give us the courage to unquestioningly obey His commands.

Just think of what the disciples had learned to know of the power of Christ Jesus here on earth. And yet that was such a little thing compared with the greater works that He was now to do in and through them. (See John 14:12.) He has the power to work even in the feeblest of His servants with the strength of the almighty God.

He has power even to use their apparent powerlessness to carry out His purposes. He has the power over every enemy and every human heart, over every difficulty and danger.

But let us remember that this power is never meant to be experienced as if it were our own. Only as Jesus Christ as a living person dwells and works with His divine energy in our own hearts and lives can there be any power in our preaching as a personal testimony. It was when Christ had said to Paul, *"My strength is made perfect in weakness"* (2 Corinthians 12:9), that Paul could say what he never learned to say before: *"When I am weak, then am I strong"* (verse 10).

The disciple of Christ who fully understands that all power has been entrusted to Christ, to be received from Him hour by hour, is the disciple who will feel the need and experience the power of these precious words: *"Lo, I am with you always"* (Matthew 28:20). Yes, the Almighty One is with us!

— 63 —

THE OMNIPRESENCE
OF CHRIST

Certainly I will be with thee.
—Exodus 3:12

The first thought of man when he imagines a god is that of power, however limited. The first thought of the true God, in contrast, is His omnipotence: *"I am God Almighty"* (Genesis 35:11). The second thought is God's omnipresence. God always gave His servants the promise of His unseen presence with them. To His *"I am with thee"* (Genesis 26:24), their faith responded, *"Thou art with me"* (Psalm 23:4).

When Christ said to His disciples, *"All power is given unto me in heaven and in earth"* (Matthew 28:18), the promise immediately followed: *"I am with you always"* (verse 20). The Omnipotent One is surely the Omnipresent One.

The psalmist spoke of God's omnipresence as something beyond his comprehension: *"Such knowledge is too wonderful for me; it is high, I cannot attain unto it"* (Psalm 139:6).

The revelation of God's omnipresence in the Man Christ Jesus makes the mystery still deeper. It also makes the grace that enables us to claim this presence as our strength and our joy something inexpressibly blessed. Yet how many servants of Christ, when the promise is given to them, find it difficult to understand all that is implied in it and how it can become the experience of their daily lives!

Here, as elsewhere in the spiritual life, everything depends on faith, on accepting Christ's words as a divine reality, and on trusting the Holy Spirit to make it true to us from moment to moment.

When Christ said He is with us always, He meant to assure us that there is not a day of our lives in which that blessed presence is not with us. It is ours every day and all day long. There does not need to be a moment in which that presence cannot be our experience. This does not depend on what we can do, but on what He undertakes to do. The omnipotent Christ is the omnipresent Christ; the ever-present is the everlasting. As surely as He is the Unchangeable One, His presence, as the power of an endless life, will be with each of His servants who trusts Him for it.

"Rest in the Lord, and wait patiently for him" (Psalm 37:7). *"Lo, I am with you always, even unto the end of the world"* (Matthew 28:20). Let your faith in Christ, the Omnipresent One, be in the quiet confidence that He will every day and every moment keep you as the apple of His eye (see Psalms 17:8), in perfect peace and in the sure experience of all the light and strength you need in His service.

CHRIST, THE SAVIOR
OF THE WORLD

This is indeed the Christ, the Saviour of the world.
—John 4:42

Omnipotence and omnipresence are considered natural attributes of God. They have their true worth only when linked to and inspired by His moral attributes of holiness and love. When our Lord spoke of the omnipotence and omnipresence that had been given to Him—*"All power...in heaven and in earth"* (Matthew 28:18); *"Lo, I am with you always"* (verse 20)—His words pointed to what lies at the root of all: His divine glory as the Savior of the world and the Redeemer of men.

> *He humbled himself, and became obedient unto death, even the death of the cross. Wherefore God also hath highly exalted him.* (Philippians 2:8–9)

While Christ was on earth, His share in the attributes of God was owing to the work He had done in His perfect obedience to the will of God and the finished redemption He had worked out for the salvation of men.

It is this that gives meaning and worth to what He said of Himself as the Omnipotent and Omnipresent One. Between His mention of these two attributes, He gave His command that they should go out into all the world and preach the gospel: *"Go ye therefore, and teach all nations, baptizing them in the name of the Father, and of the Son, and of the Holy Ghost: teaching them to observe all things whatsoever I have commanded you"* (Matthew 28:19–20). As the Redeemer who saves and keeps us from sin, as the Lord who requires obedience to all that He has commanded, He promises His divine presence to be with His servants.

Of course, only when His servants show that they obey Him in all His commands can they expect the fullness of His power and presence to be with them. Only when they themselves are living witnesses to the reality of His power to save and to keep from sin can they expect the full experience of His abiding presence and will they have power to demonstrate to others the life of obedience that He asks.

Yes, it is Jesus Christ who saves His people from their sin, who rules over a people who volunteer themselves in the day of His power (see Psalms 110:3), who proves in them that He enables them to say, *"I delight to do thy will, O my God"* (Psalm 40:8), and who says, *"Lo, I am with you always"* (Matthew 28:20). The abiding presence of the Savior is promised to all who have accepted Him in the fullness of His redeeming power from sin and who preach by their lives as well as by their words what a wonderful Savior He is.

— 65 —

CHRIST CRUCIFIED

But God forbid that I should glory, save in the
cross of our Lord Jesus Christ, by whom the world is
crucified unto me, and I unto the world.
—Galatians 6:14

Christ's highest glory is His cross. It was in this that He glorified the Father, and the Father glorified Him. In the fifth chapter of Revelation, it is as the Lamb slain in the midst of the throne that He receives the worship of the ransomed, the angels, and all creation. And it is because He is the Crucified One that His servants have learned to say, *"But God forbid that I should glory, save in the cross of our Lord Jesus Christ, by whom the world is crucified unto me, and I unto the world."* Is it not reasonable that Christ's highest glory should be our only glory, too?

When the Lord Jesus said to His disciples, *"Lo, I am with you always"* (Matthew 28:20), He gave the promise as the Crucified One, who had shown them His pierced hands and feet. And each one who seeks to claim the promise must realize that it is the crucified Jesus who promises, who offers, to be with him every day.

We do not glory in the cross by which we are crucified to the world. Is this not one of the reasons why we find it so difficult to expect and enjoy the abiding presence of Christ? We have been *"crucified with Christ"* (Galatians 2:20); our *"old man is crucified with him"* (Romans 6:6); and *"they that are Christ's have crucified the flesh with the affections and lusts"* (Galatians 5:24). Yet how little we have learned that the world has been crucified to us, and that we are free from its power. How little we have learned, as those who are crucified with Christ, to deny ourselves and have the mind that was in Christ when He took *"the form of a servant, and...humbled Himself and became obedient unto...the death of the cross"* (Philippians 2:7–8).

Oh, let us learn the lesson: it is the crucified Christ who comes to walk with us every day and in whose power we, too, are to live the life that can say, *"I am crucified with Christ...Christ* [crucified] *liveth in me"* (Galatians 2:20).

66

CHRIST GLORIFIED

The Lamb which is in the midst of the throne shall feed them.
—Revelation 7:17

*These are they which follow the Lamb
whithersoever he goeth.*
—Revelation 14:4

L*o, I am with you always*" (Matthew 28:20). Who spoke these words? We must take time to know Him well if we are to understand what we may expect from Him as He offers to be with us all day long. Who is He? None other than the Lamb standing "*in the midst of the throne…as it had been slain*" (Revelation 5:6). He is the Lamb in His deepest humiliation, enthroned in the glory of God. This is He who speaks and invites us to the closest fellowship and likeness to Himself.

It takes time, deep reverence, and adoring worship to fully understand what it means that He who dwells in the glory of the Father, before whom all heaven bows in prostrate adoration, is none other than He who offers to be your companion, to lead you like a shepherd who cares for each individual sheep, and so to make you one of those "*which follow the Lamb whithersoever he goeth.*"

Read and reread the fifth chapter of Revelation until your heart is filled with the thought of how all heaven falls prostrate, how the elders "*cast their crowns before the throne*" (Revelation 4:10), and how the Lamb reigns amid the praises and the love of His ransomed ones and all creation. If this is He who comes to you in your daily life and offers to walk with you, to be your strength, your joy, and your almighty Keeper, surely you cannot expect Him to abide with you unless your heart bows in a still deeper reverence and in a surrender to a life of praise and service that may be worthy of the love that has redeemed you.

O Christian, the Lamb in the midst of the throne is indeed the embodiment of the omnipotent glory of the everlasting God and of His love. To have this Lamb of God as your almighty Shepherd and your faithful Keeper does indeed make it possible that the thoughts and cares of earth will not separate you from His love for a single moment. (See Romans 8:38–39.)

67

CHRIST MANIFESTING HIMSELF

He that hath my commandments, and keepeth them, he it is that loveth me: and he that loveth me shall be loved of my Father, and I will love him, and will manifest myself to him.
—John 14:21

Christ had promised the disciples that the Holy Spirit would come to reveal His presence and would always be with them. When the Spirit came, Christ through the Spirit would manifest Himself to them. They would know Him in a new, divine, spiritual way; in the power of the Spirit they would know Him, and He would be far more intimately and unceasingly with them than ever He had been on earth.

The condition of this revelation of Himself is comprised in the word love: *"He that hath my commandments, and keepeth them, he it is that loveth me: and he that loveth me shall be loved of my Father, and I will love him."* This is to be the meeting of divine and human love. The love with which Christ had loved them had taken possession of their hearts and would show itself in the love for a full and absolute obedience. The Father would see this, and His love would rest upon the soul; Christ would love him with the special love drawn out by the loving heart and would manifest Himself. The love of heaven poured out in the heart (see Romans 5:5) would be met by the new and blessed revelation of Christ Himself.

But this is not all. When the question was asked, *"How is it that thou wilt manifest thyself unto us?"* (John 14:22), Jesus replied, *"If a man love me, he will keep my words: and my Father will love him, and we will come unto him, and make our abode with him"* (verse 23). In a fully surrendered heart, prepared by the Holy Spirit and showing itself in loving obedience, the Father and the Son will make their residence.

And now, Christ promised them nothing less: *"Lo, I am with you always"* (Matthew 28:20). That means Christ with the Father dwelling in the heart by faith. Oh, that everyone who wishes to enter into the secret of the abiding presence would study, believe, and claim in childlike simplicity the blessed promise: *"I will…manifest myself to him"*!

68

MARY: THE MORNING WATCH

Jesus saith unto her, Mary. She turned herself,
and saith unto him, Rabboni; which is to say, Master.
—John 20:16

Here we have the first manifestation of the risen Savior, to Mary Magdalene, the woman who *"loved much"* (Luke 7:47).

Think of what the morning watch meant to Mary. Is it not evidence of the intense longing of a love that would not rest until it had found the Lord it sought? It meant a separation from all else, even from the chief of the apostles, in her longing to find Christ. It meant the struggle of fear against a faith that refused to let go its hold of a wonderful promise. It meant Christ's coming and fulfilling the promise: *"If a man love me, he will keep my words"* and *"I will love him, and will manifest myself to him"* (John 14:23, 21). It meant that Mary's love was met by the love of Jesus, and she found Him, the living Lord, in all the power of His resurrection life. It meant that she now understood what He had said about ascending to the Father, to the life of divine and omnipotent glory. It meant, too, that she received her commission from her Lord to go and tell His disciples of what she had heard from Him.

That first morning watch, waiting for the risen Lord to reveal Himself, became a prophecy and a pledge of what the morning watch has been to thousands of souls since! In fear and doubt, and yet with a burning love and strong hope, they waited until He breathed on them the power of His resurrection life and manifested Himself as the Lord of glory. They had scarcely known Him because of their feeble human understanding; but when He breathed on them, they learned—not in words or thought, but in the reality of a divine experience—that He to whom had been given *"all power…in heaven and in earth"* (Matthew 28:18) had now taken them into the keeping of His abiding presence.

And what are we now to learn? That there is nothing that can prove a greater attraction to our Lord than the love that sacrifices everything to Him and rests satisfied with nothing less than Himself. It is to such a love that Christ manifests Himself. He *"loved us and* [has] *given himself for us"* (Ephesians 5:2). Christ's love needs our love in which to reveal itself. It is to our love that He speaks the words, *"Lo, I am with you always"* (Matthew 28:20). It is love that accepts, rejoices in, and lives in that word.

69

EMMAUS:
THE EVENING PRAYER

They constrained him, saying, Abide with us....
And he went in to tarry with them. And it came to pass,
as he sat at meat with them, he took bread, and blessed it,
and [broke it], and gave to them. And their eyes were opened,
and they knew him.
—Luke 24:29–31

Mary taught us what the morning watch can be for the revelation of Jesus to the soul. Emmaus reminds us of the place that the evening prayer may have in preparing for the full manifestation of Christ in the soul.

To the two disciples on the way to Emmaus, the day had begun in thick darkness. When they finally heard about the angel who had said that Jesus was alive, they did not know what to think. When *"Jesus himself drew near"* (verse 15), their eyes were blinded, and they did not recognize Him (verse 16). How often Jesus comes near to us with the purpose of manifesting Himself but is hindered because we are so slow to believe what the Word has spoken! But as the Lord talked with the two disciples, their hearts began to burn within them...and yet they never once thought that it might be Him. It is often the same with us today. The Word becomes precious to us in the fellowship of the saints; our hearts are stirred with the new vision of what Christ's presence may be; and yet our eyes are blinded, and we do not see Him.

When the Lord acted as though He would have gone farther, their request, *"Abide with us,"* constrained Him. On His last night, Christ had given a new meaning to the word abide. They did not yet understand this, but by using the word they received far more than they expected—a foretaste of the life of abiding, which the resurrection had now made possible. Let us learn the lesson of how necessary it is that, toward the close of each day, there should be a pause, perhaps in fellowship with others, when the whole heart takes up anew the promise of the abiding presence of Christ and prays with the urgency that constrains Him: *"Abide with us."*

And what is the chief lesson of the story? What was it that led our Lord to reveal Himself to these two men? Nothing less than their intense devotion to Him. There may be much ignorance and unbelief, but if there is a burning desire for Him above everything else—a desire that is always fostered as the Word is heard or spoken—we may be assured that He will make Himself known to us. To such intense devotion and constraining prayer, the Lord's message will be given in power: *"Lo, I am with you always"* (Matthew 28:20). Our eyes will be opened, and we will know Him and the blessed secret of the ever-abiding presence.

— 70 —

THE DISCIPLES:
THEIR DIVINE MISSION

Then the same day at evening…when the doors were shut where
the disciples were assembled for fear of the Jews,
came Jesus and stood in the midst,
and saith unto them, Peace be unto you.
—John 20:19

The disciples had received the message of Mary. Peter had told them that he had seen the Lord. Late in the evening, the men from Emmaus told how He had been made known to them. The disciples' hearts were prepared for what now came, when Jesus stood in the midst of them and said, "Peace be with you," and showed them His hands and His feet. This was to be not only a sign of recognition, but also the deep eternal mystery of what would be seen in heaven when He was standing *"in the midst of the throne…[as] a Lamb as it had been slain"* (Revelation 5:6).

"Then were the disciples glad, when they saw the LORD" (John 20:20). And He spoke again: *"Peace be unto you: as my Father hath sent me, even so send I you"* (verse 21). With Mary, He revealed Himself to the fervent love that could not rest without Him. With the men at Emmaus, it was their constraining request that received the revelation. Here He met the willing servants whom He had trained for His service, and He handed over to them the work He had done on earth. He changed their fear into the boldness of peace and gladness. He ascended to the Father; the work the Father had given Him to do He

now entrusted to them. The divine mission was now theirs to make known and carry out to victory.

For this divine work they needed nothing less than divine power. He breathed upon them the resurrection life He had won by His death. He fulfilled the promise He gave: *"Because I live, ye shall live also"* (John 14:19). The *"exceeding greatness of...power"* (Ephesians 1:19) by which God raised Christ from the dead was the same spirit of holiness by which Christ, as the Son of God, was raised from the dead and would work in them. And all that was bound or loosed in that power would be bound or loosed in heaven. (See Matthew 16:19.)

The story comes to every messenger of the gospel with wonderful power. Christ says the same words to us: *"As my Father hath sent me, even so send I you....Receive ye the Holy Ghost"* (John 20:21–22). We can have the same personal manifestation of Jesus as the Living One, with His pierced hands and feet. If our hearts are set on nothing less than the presence of the living Lord, we may be assured that it will be given to us. Jesus never sends His servants out without the promise of His abiding presence and His almighty power.

71

THOMAS: THE BLESSEDNESS OF BELIEVING

Jesus saith unto him, Thomas, because thou hast seen me, thou hast believed: blessed are they that have not seen, and yet have believed.
—John 20:29

We all consider the blessedness of Thomas as something very wonderful—Christ manifesting Himself and allowing Thomas to touch His hands and His side. It is no wonder that this blessedness could find no words except those of holy adoration: "*My LORD and my God*" (verse 28). Has there ever been a higher expression of the overwhelming nearness and glory of God?

And yet Christ said, "*Because thou hast seen me, thou hast believed: blessed are they that have not seen, and yet have believed.*" True and living faith gives a sense of Christ's divine nearness far deeper and more intimate than even the joy that filled the heart of Thomas. Here, even now, after the lapse of all these centuries, we may experience the presence and power of Christ in a far deeper reality than Thomas did. "*They that have not seen, and yet have believed*"—those who believe simply, truly, and fully in what Christ is and can be to them every moment—to these He has promised that He will manifest Himself, that the Father and He will come and dwell in them. (See John 14:21, 23.)

Have we not often been inclined to think of this full life of faith as something beyond our reach? Such a thought robs us of the power to believe. Let us turn to take hold of Christ's word: *"Blessed are they that have not seen, and yet have believed."* This is indeed the heavenly blessing, filling the whole heart and life—the faith that receives the love and the presence of the living Lord.

You ask how you may obtain this childlike faith. The answer is very simple. Where Jesus Christ is the one object of our desire and our confidence, He will manifest Himself in divine power. Thomas had proved his intense devotion to Christ when he said, *"Let us also go, that we may die with him"* (John 11:16). To such a love, even when it is struggling with unbelief, Jesus Christ will manifest Himself. He will make His holy promise an actual reality in our conscious experience: *"Lo, I am with you always"* (Matthew 28:20). Let us see to it that our faith in His blessed Word, His divine power, and His holy abiding presence is the one thing that masters our whole beings. Then Christ will indeed manifest Himself, abide with us, and dwell in our hearts as His home.

72

PETER: THE GREATNESS OF LOVE

Peter was grieved because he said unto him the third time,
Lovest thou me? And he said unto him, Lord,
thou knowest all things; thou knowest that I love thee.
Jesus saith unto him, Feed my sheep.
—John 21:17

It was to Mary, who *"loved much"* (Luke 7:47), that Christ first revealed Himself. He also revealed Himself in Peter's first vision (see John 21:1–14), to the two disciples on the road to Emmaus (see Luke 24:13–31), in His appearance to the ten (see John 20:19–23), and in the revelation of Himself to Thomas (verses 24–28). It was always to the intense devotion of a prepared heart that Christ manifested Himself. And here in His manifestation of Himself to Peter, love is again the keynote.

We can easily understand why Christ asked the question three times, *"Lovest thou me?"* It was to remind Peter of the terrible self-confidence in which he had said, *"Though I should die with thee, yet will I not deny thee"* (Matthew 26:35); of the need for quiet, deep heart-searching before he could be sure that his love was real and true; of the need for deep penitence in the consciousness of how little he could trust himself; and then of love being the one thing needed for the full restoration to his place in the heart of Jesus, the first condition for feeding His sheep and caring for His lambs.

"*God is love*" (1 John 4:8). Christ is the Son of His love. "*Having loved his own which were in the world, he loved them unto the end*" (John 13:1) and said, "*As the Father hath loved me, so have I loved you*" (John 15:9). He asked them to prove their love to Him by keeping His commandments and by loving each other with the love with which He loved them (verses 10, 12). In heaven and on earth, in the Father and in the Son, in us, in all our work for Him, and in our care for souls, the greatest thing is love.

To everyone who desires to have Jesus manifest Himself, the prerequisite is love. Peter taught us that such love is not in our power to offer. But such love came to him through the power of Christ's death to sin—the power of His resurrection life, of which Peter became partaker. Peter said in his first epistle, "*Whom having not seen, ye love; in whom, though now ye see him not, yet believing, ye rejoice with joy unspeakable and full of glory*" (1 Peter 1:8). Thank God, if Peter could be so changed, Christ will certainly work the wondrous change in us, too, and will manifest Himself to a loving heart in all the fullness of His precious word: "*Lo, I am with you always*" (Matthew 28:20). Such love, to which Christ will reveal Himself, is the only preparation for feeding His sheep and tending His lambs.

73

JOHN: LIFE FROM THE DEAD

And when I saw him, I fell at his feet as dead. And he laid his
right hand upon me, saying unto me, Fear not;
I am the first and the last: I am he that liveth, and was dead;
and, behold, I am alive for evermore.
—Revelation 1:17–18

Here we have Christ manifesting Himself, sixty or more years after the resurrection, to the beloved disciple. John "*fell at His feet as dead.*" In answer to Moses's prayer for God to show him His glory (Exodus 33:18), God had said to him, "*Thou canst not see my face: for there shall no man see me, and live*" (verse 20). Man's sinful nature cannot receive the vision of the divine glory and live; it needs the death of the natural life for the life of God in glory to enter in. When John fell at Christ's feet "*as dead,*" it proved how little he could endure the wonderful heavenly vision.

When Christ laid His right hand upon John and said, "*Fear not...I am he that liveth, and was dead; and, behold, I am alive for evermore,*" He reminded John that He Himself had passed through death before He could rise to the life and glory of God. For the Master Himself and for every disciple, for Moses and for John, there is only one way to the glory of God. That way consists of death to all the nature that has been in contact with sin and cannot enter heaven.

This lesson is a deep and necessary one for all who desire Jesus to manifest Himself to them. The knowledge of Jesus, fellowship with Him, and the experience of His power are not possible without the sacrifice of all that is worldly in us. The disciples experienced this. When Christ spoke about forsaking one's father and mother, about taking up the cross, about losing one's life for His sake—in everything He said, down to the days before His death, when He said, *"Except a corn of wheat fall into the ground and die, it abideth alone: but if it die, it bringeth forth much fruit. He that loveth his life shall lose it"* (John 12:24–25)—He made this the one great charge: deny self; bear the cross, and follow Me.

What is the secret of obtaining the abiding presence of the Lord Jesus as our daily portion? Let us accept the lesson—through death to life. In the power of Christ Jesus, with whom we have been crucified and whose death now works in us, if we will yield ourselves to it, death to sin and to the world is to be the deepest law of our spiritual lives. The disciples had followed Christ to the cross. That was what prepared them to receive the Master's words: *"Lo, I am with you always"* (Matthew 28:20).

— 74 —

PAUL: CHRIST REVEALED
IN HIM

It pleased God…to reveal his Son in me.
—Galatians 1:15–16

In all our study and worship of Christ, we find our thoughts gathering round these five points: the incarnate Christ, the crucified Christ, the enthroned Christ, the indwelling Christ, and Christ coming in glory. If the first is the seed, the second is the seed cast into the ground, and the third is the seed growing up to heaven. Then follows the fruit through the Holy Spirit, which is Christ dwelling in the heart, and then the gathering of the fruit when Christ appears.

Paul told us that it pleased God to reveal His Son in him. And he gave his testimony of the result of that revelation: *"I am crucified with Christ: nevertheless I live; yet not I, but Christ liveth in me"* (Galatians 2:20). In Christ, he had found the death of self. Just as the cross is the chief characteristic of Christ Himself—*"in the midst of the throne… stood a Lamb as it had been slain"* (Revelation 5:6)—so the life of Christ in Paul made him inseparably one with his crucified Lord. So completely was this the case that he could say, *"But God forbid that I should glory, save in the cross of our Lord Jesus Christ, by whom the world is crucified unto me, and I unto the world"* (Galatians 6:14).

If you had asked Paul, "If Christ so actually lives in you that you no longer live, what responsibility do you have in living your life?" the answer was ready and clear: *"I live by the faith of the Son of God, who loved me, and gave himself for me"* (Galatians 2:20). His life was every moment a life of faith in Him who had loved him and given Himself completely. Christ had undertaken at all times to be the life of His willing disciple.

This was the sum and substance of all Paul's teaching. He asked for intercession so that he might speak *"the mystery of Christ"* (Colossians 4:3), *"the riches of the glory of this mystery among the Gentiles; which is Christ in you, the hope of glory"* (Colossians 1:27). The indwelling Christ was the secret of his life of faith, the one power, the one aim of all his life and work, *"the hope of glory."* Let us believe in the abiding presence of Christ as the sure gift to each one who trusts Him fully.

75

WHY COULD WE NOT?

Then came the disciples to Jesus apart, and said,
Why could not we cast him out? And Jesus said unto them,
Because of your unbelief.…Howbeit this kind goeth not out but
by prayer and fasting.
—Matthew 17:19–21

The disciples had often cast out devils, but here they had been powerless. They asked the Lord what the reason might be. His answer
was very simple: *"Because of your unbelief."*

We have here the reply to the question that is so often asked,
"Why can't we live the life of unbroken fellowship with Christ that
the Scriptures promise?" Simply because of our unbelief. We do
not realize that faith must *accept* and *expect* that God will, by His
almighty power, fulfill every promise He has made. We do not live
in the utter helplessness and dependence on God alone that is the
very essence of faith. We are not *"strong in faith…fully persuaded that,*
what he [God] had promised, he was able also to perform" (Romans
4:20–21). We do not give ourselves with our whole hearts to believe
that God, by His almighty power, will work wonders in our hearts.

But what can be the reason that this faith is so often lacking?
"Howbeit this kind goeth not out but by prayer and fasting." A strong
faith in God needs a life in close touch with Him by persistent prayer.
We cannot call up faith at our bidding; it requires close fellowship
with God. It requires not only prayer, but also fasting, in the larger
and deeper meaning of that word. It requires the denial of self, the

sacrifice of pleasing of *"the lust of the flesh, and the lust of the eyes, and the pride of life"* (1 John 2:16), which are the essence of a worldly spirit. To gain the prizes of the heavenly life here on earth, one needs to sacrifice all that earth can offer. Just as one needs God to satisfy the human heart and work His mighty miracles in it, the whole man must be utterly given up to God in order to have the power of the faith that can cast out every evil spirit. *"Prayer and fasting"* are essential.

76

THE POWER OF OBEDIENCE

And he that sent me is with me: the Father hath not left me
alone; for I do always those things that please him.
—John 8:29

In these words, Christ not only tells what His life with the Father was, but He also reveals at the same time the law of all communion with God—simple obedience.

We see in the Farewell Discourses how strongly Christ insisted upon it. He said, *"If ye love me, keep my commandments. And I will pray the Father, and he shall give you another Comforter* [the Holy Spirit]*"* (John 14:15–16). He stressed this point twice more: *"And he that loveth me shall be loved of my Father, and I will love him, and will manifest myself to him"* (verse 21); *"And we will come unto him, and make our abode with him"* (verse 23). Christ also mentioned obedience three times in chapter 15: *"If…my words abide in you, ye shall ask what ye will, and it shall be done unto you"* (verse 7); *"If ye keep my commandments, ye shall abide in my love; even as I have kept my Father's commandments, and abide in his love"* (verse 10); *"Ye are my friends, if ye do whatsoever I command you"* (verse 14).

Obedience is the proof and the exercise of the love of God that has been *"shed abroad in our hearts by the Holy Ghost"* (Romans 5:5). It comes from love and leads to love, a deeper and a fuller experience of God's love and indwelling. It assures us that what we ask will be given to us. It assures us that we are abiding in the love of Christ. It seals our claim to be called the friends of Christ. And so it is not only a proof of love, but also of faith, as assuring us that *"whatsoever we ask, we receive of him, because we keep his commandments, and do those things that are pleasing in his sight"* (1 John 3:22).

For the abiding enjoyment of the holy presence, simple, full obedience is necessary. The new covenant has made full provision for this: *"I will put my law in their inward parts, and write it in their hearts"* (Jeremiah 31:33); "I will put my fear in their hearts, that they shall not depart from me" (Jeremiah 32:40); *"I will put my spirit within you, and cause you to walk in my statutes, and ye shall keep my judgments, and do them"* (Ezekiel 36:27).

Obedience enables us to abide in His love and gives us the full experience of His unbroken presence. Christ did not speak of an impossibility; He saw what we might confidently expect in the power of the Spirit. Remember, it is to the obedient disciple that Christ says, *"Lo, I am with you always"* (Matthew 28:20), and to whom all the fullness of its meaning will be revealed.

77

THE POWER OF INTERCESSION

We will give ourselves continually to prayer.
—Acts 6:4

*Prayer was made without ceasing of the
church unto God for him.*
—Acts 12:5

Dr. John R. Mott, an American Methodist leader, urged us to believe in the unlimited power of united intercession. While travelling in Asia, he was charged to press upon the missionary societies the imperative need of more intercession—above all, of united intercession. He wrote:

> In no way can we so well serve, the deepest interests of all the societies, missions, and Churches as by multiplying the number of real intercessors, and by focusing the prayers of Christendom upon those great situations, wonderful openings, grave crises, alarming perils and remarkable movements which demand the almighty working of the Spirit of God....Far more important and vital than any service we can render...is that of helping to release the superhuman energies of prayer, and, through uniting in this holy ministry true intercessors of all lands and of all communions, of helping to usher in a new era abounding in signs and wonders characteristic of the working of the Living Christ. We should be on our guard lest we devote a disproportionate amount of time

and thought to investigation and discussion and to plans for the utilization of available human forces, and not enough attention to what is immeasurably more important—the relating of what we do personally and corporately to the fountain of divine life and energy. The Christian world has a right to expect from the leaders of the missionary forces not only a more thorough handling of the facts and methods, but also a larger discovery of superhuman resources and a greater irradiation of spiritual power.[4]

And where is there a greater need of focusing the united intercession of Christendom than on the great army of missionaries, of whom I wrote in the introduction to this section? They confess the need for the presence and the power of God's Spirit in their lives and work. They long for the experience of the abiding presence and power of Christ every day. They need it; they have a right to it. Will you, my dear reader, be a part of the great army that pleads with God for that infilling of power that is so absolutely necessary for effective work? Will you, like the early church, give yourself *"continually to prayer"* (Acts 6:4), until God sends an abundant answer? As we pray *"without ceasing"* (Acts 12:5), the power of the promise, *"Lo, I am with you always"* (Matthew 28:20), will be proved in our lives.

---

4. John R. Mott, "Present Possibilities of Co-operation in the Mission Field," *The International Review of Missions*, April 1914, 224.

78

THE POWER OF TIME

My times are in thy hand.
—Psalm 31:15

The plural in this Scripture verse implies the singular: "All my time is in Your hands, O God. It belongs to You; You alone have the right to command it. I yield it wholly and gladly to Your disposal." What mighty power time can exert if wholly given up to God!

Time is lord of all things. What is all the history of the world if not proof of how, slowly but surely, time has made man what he is today? All around us we see the evidence. In the success of every pursuit, in all our efforts and accomplishments, it is under the law of time and its inconceivable power that we spend our lives.

This is especially true in religion and in our fellowship with God. Time is master here, too. Our communion with God, our likeness to His image, and our power in His service all depend on one condition: that we have sufficient time with God for His holiness to shine on us with its light and to make us partakers of His Spirit and His life. The very essence of religion lies in how much time we spend with God. Yet so many of God's servants, while giving their lives to His service, frankly confess that the feebleness of their spiritual lives and the inadequate results of their mission work as a whole are due to the failure to make time for daily communion with God—and to use it wisely.

What can be the cause of this sad confession? Nothing but a lack of faith in the Godgiven assurance that time spent alone with Him will indeed bring into the lives of His servants the power to enable them to use all their time in His fellowship. Then His abiding presence will be with them all day long.

O my fellow Christian, you complain that you are overworked, or that your zeal hinders your spiritual effectiveness. Do you not see that if you would only submit your time to the inspection of Christ and His Holy Spirit, you would find that a new life would be yours if you fully believed and put into practice this Scripture: *"My times are in thy hand"*?

79

THE POWER OF FAITH

All things are possible to him that believeth.
—Mark 9:23

Scripture teaches us that there is not one truth on which Christ insisted more frequently, both with His disciples and with those who came seeking His help, than the absolute necessity of faith and its unlimited possibilities. And experience has taught us that there is nothing in which we come so short as the simple and absolute trust in God to literally fulfill in us all that He has promised. A life in the abiding presence must be a life of unceasing faith.

Think for a moment of the marks of a true faith. First of all, faith depends on God to do all that He has promised. A person with true faith does not rest content with taking some of the promises; he seeks nothing less than to claim every promise that God has made in its largest and fullest meaning. Under a sense of the nothingness and utter powerlessness of his faith, he trusts the power of an almighty God to work wonders in the heart in which He dwells.

The person of faith does this with his whole heart and all his strength. His faith yields to the promise that God will take full possession, and throughout the day and night will inspire his hope and expectation. By faith, he recognizes the inseparable link that unites God's promises and His commands, and he yields to do the one as fully as he trusts the other.

In the pursuit of the power that such a life of faith can give, there is often a faith that seeks and strives but cannot grasp. This is followed by a faith that begins to see that waiting on God is needed, and quietly rests in the hope of what God will do. This should lead to an act of decision, in which the soul takes God at His Word, claims the fulfillment of the promise, and then looks to Him, even in utter darkness, to perform what He has spoken.

The life of faith to which the abiding presence will be granted must have complete mastery of the whole being. It is such a wonderful privilege—Christ's presence actually keeping us all day long in its blessedness—that it needs a parting with much that was formerly thought lawful, if He is indeed to be the Lord of all, the blessed Friend who is our companion, the joy and light of our lives. By such faith, we will be able to claim and experience the words of the Master: *"Lo, I am with you always"* (Matthew 28:20).

— 80 —

JOHN'S MISSIONARY MESSAGE

That which we have seen and heard declare we unto you,
that ye also may have fellowship with us: and truly our
fellowship is with the Father, and with his Son Jesus Christ.
—1 John 1:3

What a revelation of the calling placed on every preacher of the gospel! His message is nothing less than to proclaim that Christ has opened the way for us to have daily, living, loving fellowship with the holy God. He is to preach this as a witness to the life he himself lives in all its blessed experience. In the power of that testimony, he is to prove its reality and show how a sinful man upon earth can indeed live in fellowship with the Father and the Son.

The message suggests to us that the very first duty of the missionary every day of his life is to maintain such close communion with God that he can preach the truth in the fullness of joy, with the knowledge that his life and conversation are the proof that his preaching is true, so that his words appeal with power to the heart: *"And these things write we unto you, that your joy may be full"* (verse 4).

The October 1914 issue of *The International Review of Missions* contained an article on the influence of the Keswick Convention on mission work. Keswick is well-known as the English town in which a great revival began. The article provides the substance of Keswick teaching in these words:

The possibilities of attainment in the Christian life were unfolded from the New Testament and applied in a practical way: this involved no teaching of sinlessness, but it pointed to a life of communion with God through Christ as a reality to be entered upon and constantly maintained. The entrance on such a life and the continuance in it were shown to depend upon the unconditional and habitual surrender of the whole personality to Christ's control and government, and on the assurance that the living Christ would take possession of the life thus yielded to Him.[5]

It is such teaching, revealing the infinite claim and power of Christ's love as maintained by the power of the Holy Spirit that will encourage and compel men to make the measure of Christ's surrender for them the only measure of their surrender to Him and His service.

It is this intimate fellowship with Christ as the secret of daily service and testimony that has power to make Christ known as the Deliverer from sin and the inspiration of a life of wholehearted devotion to His service. It is this intimate and abiding fellowship with Christ that the promise, *"Lo, I am with you always"* (Matthew 28:20), secures for us. This is what every missionary needs, what every missionary has a right to claim. By this alone, he maintains the spiritual effectiveness that will influence the workers and the converts with whom he comes into contact.

---

5. Walter B. Sloan, "The Influence of the Keswick Convention on Missionary Work," *The International Review of Missions*, 709.

81

PAUL'S MISSIONARY MESSAGE

Continue in prayer…Withal praying also for us, that God
would open unto us a door of utterance, to speak the mystery of
Christ…that I may make it manifest, as I ought to speak.
—Colossians 4:2–4

The mystery which…now is made manifest to his saints:
to whom God would make known
what is the riches of the glory of this mystery among the
Gentiles; which is Christ in you, the hope of glory.
—Colossians 1:26–27

To Paul, the very center and substance of his gospel was the indwelling Christ. He spoke of the *"riches of the glory of this mystery… Christ in you, the hope of glory."* Though he had been a preacher of this gospel for so many years, he still asked for prayer so that he might correctly make known the mystery of it.

I often hear complaints that, after a time, there appears to be no further growth in many churches, and very little of the joy and power for bearing witness to Christ Jesus. The question arises whether the home church is living in the experience of the indwelling Christ, so that the missionaries whom she sends out know the secret and make it the substance of their message.

Some years ago, I knew a minister who went to the mission field. Before he left, there was a little gathering for prayer, at which he asked what his message should be. The thought was expressed that, in speaking to Christians, it was desirable to present a message of a full salvation, so that people would be roused to believe in and accept an indwelling Christ. On his return, he told with what deep interest the presentation of this truth had been received, many saying that they had never before understood this.

Dr. Alexander Maclaren, a Baptist preacher, once said that it seemed as if the church had lost the truth of the indwelling Christ. We speak of Paul's missionary *methods*, but is there not a greater need for Paul's missionary *message* that culminates in the words, *"Christ in you, the hope of glory"*? Are not all missionary intercessors, and missionaries themselves, called to make it a matter of first importance to lead Christians into the enjoyment of their rightful heritage? *"If a man love me, he will keep my words: and my Father will love him, and we will come unto him, and make our abode with him"* (John 14:23). And it may be the home church that will also share in the blessing, the restoration of this truth to its right place: *"Christ in you, the hope of glory."*

82

THE MISSIONARY'S LIFE

Ye are witnesses, and God also, how holily
and righteously and unblameably we behaved ourselves toward
you that believe.
—1 Thessalonians 2:10 RV

Paul more than once appealed to what his converts had seen of his own life. He said, *"Our rejoicing is this, the testimony of our conscience, that in simplicity and godly sincerity, not with fleshly wisdom, but by the grace of God, we have had our conversation in the world, and more abundantly to you-ward"* (2 Corinthians 1:12). Christ had taught His disciples as much by His life as by His teaching. Paul had sought to be a living witness to the truth of all that he had preached about Christ— that He is able to save and to keep from sin, that He renews the whole nature by the power of His Holy Spirit, and that He Himself becomes the life of those who believe in Him.

One writer, expressing his ideas about world missions, has said, "It has come to pass that our representatives on the field, just because they are what we have made them, have far too often hidden the Christ whom they are giving their lives to reveal. Only to the degree that the missionary manifests the character of Christ in and through his own life can he gain an audience for the gospel. Only as far as he can live Christ before their eyes can he help them to understand his message."

Paul referred to his life as holy, righteous, and blameless; this gave him courage to put a high standard before his converts. In the same epistle, he called them to trust God, to establish their hearts "*unblameable in holiness before God*" (1 Thessalonians 3:13). Later in the epistle, he wrote, "*The very God of peace sanctify you wholly… who also will do it*" (1 Thessalonians 5:23–24). In Philippians 4:9, he wrote, "*Those things, which ye have both learned, and received, and heard, and seen in me, do: and the God of peace shall be with you.*" And in 1 Timothy 1:14–16 we find, "*The grace of our Lord was exceeding abundant with faith and love which is in Christ Jesus. This is…a pattern to them which should hereafter believe on him to life everlasting.*"

Let us believe that when Paul said, "Nevertheless I live; yet not I, but Christ liveth in me" (Galatians 2:20), he spoke of an actual, divine, unceasing abiding of Christ in him, working in him from hour to hour all that was well-pleasing to the Father. And let us not rest until we can say, "The Christ of Paul is my Christ! All that filled his soul from heaven is mine, too."

— 83 —

THE HOLY SPIRIT

*When he, the Spirit of truth, is come…he shall glorify me: for
he shall receive of mine, and shall [show] it unto you.*
—John 16:13–14

W hen our Lord said to the disciples, *"Lo, I am with you always"*
(Matthew 28:20), they did not at first understand or experience the
full meaning of His words. It was at Pentecost—when they were
filled with the Holy Spirit from heaven, who brought down into their
hearts the glorified Lord Jesus—that they began the new life in the
joy of the abiding presence.

All our attempts to live this life of continuous, unbroken communion will be in vain unless we too yield ourselves wholly to the
power and the indwelling of the ever-blessed Spirit. Throughout the
church of Christ, there is an apparent lack of faith in what the Spirit
is as God, in what He can enable us to be, and in how completely He
demands full and undisturbed possession of our whole beings. All
our faith in the fulfillment of Christ's glorious promises, especially
that of the Father and Son making their abode in us (see John 14:23),
is subject to one essential and indispensable condition: a life utterly
and unceasingly yielded to the rule and leading of the Spirit of Christ.

I hope no one will say, "The experience of Christ's being with us
every day and all day long is impossible." Christ meant His words to
be a simple, eternal reality. He meant the promises to be accepted as
absolute divine truth: *"He it is that loveth me: and he that loveth me
shall be loved of my Father, and I will love him, and will manifest myself*

to him" (John 14:21); "*We will come unto him, and make our abode with him*" (verse 23). But such truth can only be experienced where the Spirit, in His power as God, is known, believed in, and obeyed. What Christ spoke of in John 14 is what Paul testified of when he said, "*Christ liveth in me*" (Galatians 2:20), or, as John expressed it, "*And hereby we know that he abideth in us, by the Spirit which he hath given us*" (1 John 3:24).

Christ came as God to make known the Father, and the Spirit came as God to make known the Son in us. We need to understand that the Spirit, as God, claims absolute surrender and is willing to take possession of our whole beings and enable us to fulfill all that Christ asks of us. It is the Spirit who can deliver us from all the power of the flesh, who can conquer the power of the world in us. It is the Spirit through whom Christ Jesus will manifest Himself to us in nothing less than His abiding presence: "*Lo, I am with you always*" (Matthew 28:20).

FILLED WITH THE SPIRIT

Be filled with the Spirit; speaking to yourselves in psalms and hymns and spiritual songs, singing and making melody in your heart to the Lord; giving thanks always for all things.
—Ephesians 5:18–20

If the expression *"filled with the Spirit"* could be applied only to the story of Pentecost, we might think that it was something special and not meant for ordinary life. But the above Scripture teaches us that it is meant for every Christian and for everyday life.

To realize this more fully, think of what the Holy Spirit was in Christ Jesus and what the conditions were under which He, as man, was filled with the Spirit. He received the Spirit when He was praying and had yielded Himself as a sacrifice to God—when He was baptized in the sinner's baptism. Full of the Holy Spirit, Jesus was led to the forty days' fasting, sacrificing the needs of the body to be free for fellowship with the Father and the victory over Satan. He even refused, when He was extremely hungry, to listen to the temptation of the evil one to use His power to make bread to supply His hunger. And so He was led by the Spirit all through life until He, by the eternal Spirit, offered Himself without blemish to God. In Christ, the Spirit meant prayer, obedience, and sacrifice.

Likewise, if we are to follow Christ, to have His mind in us, and to live out His life, we must seek to regard the fullness of the Spirit as a daily supply, a daily provision. In no other way can we live the life of obedience, joy, self-sacrifice, and power for service. There may be occasions when that fullness of the Spirit will become especially manifested, but only as we are led by the Spirit every day and all day long can we abide in Christ Jesus, conquer the flesh and the world, and live the life with God in prayer and with our fellowmen in humble, holy, fruitful service.

Above all, it is only as we are filled with the Spirit that the words of Jesus can be fully understood and experienced: *"Lo, I am with you always"* (Matthew 28:20). Let no one think this is too high or that this is impossible. *"The things which are impossible with men are possible with God"* (Luke 18:27). And if we cannot attain it immediately, let us at least, in an act of holy decision, make it our definite aim, our unceasing prayer, our childlike expectation. Christ's assurance that He is with us always was meant for daily life, with the sure and allsufficient aid of the blessed Spirit. Our faith in Christ will be the measure of our fullness of the Spirit. The measure of the power of the Spirit in us will be the measure of our experience of the presence of Christ.

— 85 —

THE CHRIST LIFE

Christ…is our life.
—Colossians 3:4

Christ's life was more than His teaching, more than His work, more than even His death. It was His life in the sight of God and man that gave value to what He said, did, and suffered. And it is this life, glorified in the resurrection, that He imparts to His people and enables them to live out before men.

"By this shall all men know that ye are my disciples, if ye have love one to another" (John 13:35). It was the life in the new brotherhood of the Holy Spirit that made both Jews and Greeks feel that there was some superhuman power about Christ's disciples; they gave living proof of the truth of what they said, that God's love had come down and taken possession of them.

It has often been said that unless the missionary lives out the Christ life on an entirely different level from that on which other men live, he misses the deepest secret of power and success in his work. When Christ sent His disciples forth, it was with the command, "Tarry…until ye be endued with power from on high" (Luke 24:49); "But ye shall receive power, after that the Holy Ghost is come upon you: and ye shall be witnesses unto me…unto the uttermost part of the earth" (Acts 1:8). Many missionaries have felt that it is not learning, zeal, or the willingness for self-sacrifice in Christ's service that enables them to meet and overcome every difficulty, but the secret experience of the life "hid with Christ in God" (Colossians 3:3).

Everything depends on the life with God in Christ being right. It was so with Christ, with the disciples, and with Paul. The simplicity and intensity of our lives in Christ Jesus, and the life of Christ Jesus in us, sustains us in the daily drudgery of work, makes us conquer self and everything that could hinder the Christ life, and gives victory over the powers of evil and over the hearts from which the evil spirits have to be cast out.

The life is everything. It was so in Christ Jesus. It must be so in His servants, too. It can be so because Christ Himself will live in us. When He said, *"Lo, I am with you always"* (Matthew 28:20), He meant nothing less than this: "Every day and all day long, I am with you, the secret of your life, your joy, and your strength."

Oh, to learn what hidden treasures are contained in the blessed words we love to repeat: "Lo, I am with you all the days!"

— 86 —

THE CHRISTLIKE LIFE

Let this mind be in you, which was also in Christ Jesus.
—Philippians 2:5

What was the mind that was in Christ Jesus? He *"took upon him the form of a servant, and was made in the likeness of men: and… he humbled himself, and became obedient unto death, even the death of the cross"* (verses 7–8). Self-emptying and self-sacrifice, obedience to God's will, and love for men, even to the death of the cross—such was the character of Christ for which God so *"highly exalted him"* (verse 9). Such is the character of Christ that we are to imitate. He was made in the likeness of men, so that we might be conformed into the likeness of God.

Self-effacement, self-sacrifice, so that God's will might be done and man might be saved—such was the life of Christ. Love *"seeketh not her own"* (1 Corinthians 13:5). This was His life; He lived only to please God and to bless men.

Let no one say that this is an impossibility. *"The things which are impossible with men are possible with God"* (Luke 18:27). We are called to *"work out"* this salvation of a Christlike character *"with fear and trembling. For it is God which worketh in [us] both to will and to do of his good pleasure"* (Philippians 2:12–13). Christ said, *"The Father that dwelleth in me, he doeth the works"* (John 14:10); it is He who works in us *"to will and to do."*

It has been said that the missionary who is to commend the gospel must first embody it in a character fully conformed to the likeness of Jesus Christ. Only as far as he can live Christ before the eyes of the converts can he help them to understand his message. At times our representatives on the field, just because they are what we have made them, have far too often hidden the Christ whom they are giving their lives to reveal.

As the church aims to make some noticeable degree of likeness to Christ's character the standard for Christian teachers, our missionaries will be able to pass this on to their converts and say to them, *"Be ye followers of me, even as I also am of Christ"* (1 Corinthians 11:1).

Let us not rest until our faith lays hold of the promise, *"It is God which worketh in you"* (Philippians 2:13). The confidence will be aroused that, as the character of Christ is the revelation with which every missionary has been entrusted, so the power will be given to fulfill this high and holy calling. Let ministers, missionaries, and all intercessors make this their one great plea and aim to have this mind *"which was also in Christ Jesus"* (Philippians 2:5).

87

CHRIST, THE NEARNESS OF GOD

Draw nigh to God, and he will draw nigh to you.
—James 4:8

I t has been said that the holiness of God is the union of God's infinite distance from sinful man with His infinite nearness to man in His redeeming grace. Faith must always seek to realize both the distance and the nearness.

In Christ, God has come near, so very near to man, and now the command comes: if you want to have God come still nearer, you must draw near to Him. The promised nearness of Christ Jesus expressed in the promise, *"Lo, I am with you always"* (Matthew 28:20), can only be experienced as we draw near to Him.

This means, first of all, that we must yield ourselves afresh at the beginning of each day for His holy presence to rest upon us. It means a voluntary, intentional, and wholehearted turning away from the world, to wait on God to make Himself known to our souls. It means giving time, and all our hearts and strength, to allow Him to reveal Himself. It is impossible to expect the abiding presence of Christ with us throughout the day unless there is a definite daily exercise of strong desire and childlike trust in His word: *"Draw nigh to God, and he will draw nigh to you."*

Furthermore, this means the simple, childlike offering of ourselves and our lives in everything, in order to do His will alone and to seek above everything to please Him. His promise is sure: *"If a man love me, he will keep my words: and my Father will love him, and we will come unto him, and make our abode with him"* (John 14:23).

Then comes the quiet assurance of faith, even if there is not much feeling or sense of His presence, that God is with us and will watch over us and keep us as we go out to do His will. Moreover, He will strengthen us *"in the inner man"* (Ephesians 3:16) with divine strength for the work we have to do for Him.

Child of God, let these words come to you with a new meaning each morning: *"Draw nigh to God, and he will draw nigh to you."* Wait patiently, and He will speak in divine power: *"Lo, I am with you always"* (Matthew 28:20).

88

LOVE

Having loved his own which were in the world,
[Jesus] loved them unto the end.
—John 13:1

These are the opening words of the holy, confidential talk of Christ with His disciples, as He discoursed with them out of the depths of eternity in the last hours before He went to Gethsemane. (See John 13–17.) They are the revelation and full display of the divine love that was manifested in His death on the cross.

He began with the new commandment: "*That ye love one another; as I have loved you*" (John 13:34). Later, He told His disciples, "*If ye love me, keep my commandments.…He that loveth me shall be loved of my Father, and I will love him, and will manifest myself to him.…And we will come unto him, and make our abode with him*" (John 14:15, 21, 23). The new life, the heavenly life in Christ Jesus, is to be the unfolding of God's love in Christ. Then, farther on, we read, "*As the Father hath loved me, so have I loved you: continue ye in my love. If ye keep my commandments, ye shall abide in my love.…This is my commandment, That ye love one another, as I have loved you. Greater love hath no man than this, that a man lay down his life for his friends*" (John 15:9–10, 12–13). Then He prayed to the Father, "*That the world may know that thou hast sent me, and hast loved them, as thou hast loved me.…I have declared unto them thy name, and will declare it: that the love wherewith thou hast loved me may be in them, and I in them*" (John 17:23, 26).

Can words make it plainer that God's love for Christ is meant to pass into us and become our life, so that the love with which the Father loved the Son can be in us? If the Lord Jesus is to manifest Himself to us, it can only be to the loving heart. If we are to claim His daily presence with us, it can only be as a relationship of infinite, tender love is formed between Him and us—love rooted in the faith of God's love for Christ coming into our hearts and showing itself in obedience to His commandments and in love for one another.

In the early church, the *"first love"* (Revelation 2:4) was forsaken after a time, and confidence was put in all the activities of service instead of in God. It is only in the atmosphere of a holy, living love that the abiding presence of the loving Christ can be known, and the depth of divine love expressed in Christ's promise, *"Lo, I am with you always"* (Matthew 28:20), will be realized.

— 89 —

THE TRIAL AND TRIUMPH OF FAITH

*Jesus said unto him, If thou canst believe, all things
are possible to him that believeth. And straightway the father of
the child cried out, and said with tears, Lord,
I believe; help thou mine unbelief.*
—Mark 9:23–24

What a glorious promise: *"All things are possible to him that believeth"*! And yet it is just the greatness of this promise that constitutes the trial of faith. At first we do not really believe its truth. But when we have grasped it, then comes the real trial in the thought, "Such a wonderworking faith is utterly beyond my reach."

But what constitutes the trial of faith soon becomes its triumph. How can this be? When the father of the child heard Christ say to him, *"If thou canst believe, all things are possible to him that believeth,"* he felt that this was only casting him into deeper despair. How could his faith be able to work the miracle? But as he looked into the face of Christ, and as the love of His tender eyes touched his heart, he felt sure that this blessed Man had not only the power to heal his child, but also the power to inspire him with the needed faith. The impression Christ produced upon him made possible not only the one miracle of the healing, but also the second miracle that he should have so great a faith. And with tears he cried, *"Lord, I believe; help thou mine unbelief."* The very greatness of faith's trial was the greatness of faith's triumph.

What a lesson! Of all things that are possible to faith, we think the most impossible is that we should be able to exercise such faith. But the abiding presence of Christ is possible to faith, and this faith is possible to the soul that clings to Christ and trusts Him. As surely as He will lead us into His abiding presence all day long, so surely will He strengthen us with divine power for the faith that claims and receives the promise. Blessed is the hour when the believer sees how entirely he is dependent on Christ for the faith as well as the blessing. In the consciousness of the unbelief that is still struggling within, he casts himself on the power and the love of Jesus, saying, "Lord, I believe! Lord, I believe!"

Through such trial and through such triumph—sometimes the triumph of despair—we enter into our inheritance, which is the abiding presence of Him who speaks to us now: *"Lo, I am with you always"* (Matthew 28:20). Let us wait at His feet until we know that He has blessed us. *"I can do all things through Christ which strengtheneth me"* (Philippians 4:13).

— 90 —

EXCEEDING ABUNDANTLY

*Now unto him that is able to do exceeding abundantly above all
that we ask or think, according to the power that
worketh in us, Unto him be glory in the church by Christ Jesus
throughout all ages, world without end. Amen.*
—Ephesians 3:20–21

In the above prayer, Paul had apparently reached the highest expression possible of the life to which God's mighty power could bring the believer. But Paul was not content. In this doxology, he rose still higher and lifted us up to give glory to God as *"able to do exceeding abundantly above all that we ask or think."* Pause a moment to think what that means.

Think of the words *"exceeding great and precious promises"* (2 Peter 1:4). Think of *"the exceeding greatness of his power to us-ward who believe, according to the working of his mighty power, which he wrought in Christ, when he raised him from the dead"* (Ephesians 1:19–20). Think of *"the grace of our Lord"* as *"exceeding abundant with faith and love which is in Christ Jesus"* (1 Timothy 1:14), so that *"where sin abounded, grace did much more abound"* (Romans 5:20). He lifts our hearts to give glory to God as able to do *"do exceeding abundantly above all that we ask or think,"* according to the greatness of His power at work within us—nothing less than the power that raised Christ from the dead. And as our hearts begin to feel that this is an indication of something that God will work in us beyond all our imagination, He lifts our hearts to join in the universal chorus: *"Unto him be glory in the church by Christ Jesus throughout all ages, world without end. Amen."*

As we worship and adore, the call comes to believe in this almighty God who is working in our hearts according to His mighty power, able and willing to fulfill every one of His *"exceeding great and precious promises"* (2 Peter 1:4), and where sin abounds, to prove that grace abounds more exceedingly. (See Romans 5:20.)

Paul began his great prayer, *"I bow my knees unto the Father"* (Ephesians 3:14). He ended it by bringing us to our knees, to give glory to Him as able to fulfill every promise, to reveal Christ dwelling in our hearts, and to keep us in the life of love that leads to being *"filled with all the fulness of God"* (verse 19).

Child of God, bow in deep adoration, giving glory to God, until the prayer is fulfilled and Jesus dwells in your heart by faith. Faith in this almighty God, and the exceeding abundance of His grace and power, will teach you that the indwelling of Christ is the secret of the abiding presence.

ABOUT THE AUTHOR

Andrew Murray (1828–1917) was an amazingly prolific Christian writer who lived and ministered as both a pastor and author in the towns and villages of South Africa. Some of Murray's earliest works were an extension of his pastoral work, written to provide nurture and guidance to Christians, whether young or old in the faith. Once books such as *Abide in Christ, Divine Healing,* and *With Christ in the School of Prayer* were written, Murray became widely known, and new books from his pen were awaited with great eagerness around the world.

He wrote to give daily practical help to many of the people in his congregation who lived out in the farming communities and could come into town for church services only on rare occasions. As he wrote these books of instruction, Murray adopted the practice of placing many of his more devotional books into thirty-one separate readings to correspond with the days of the month.

At the age of seventy-eight, Murray resigned from the pastorate and devoted most of his time to his manuscripts. He continued to write profusely, moving from one book to the next with an intensity of purpose and a zeal that few men of God have ever equaled. He often said of himself, rather humorously, that he was like a hen about to hatch an egg; he was restless and unhappy until he got the burden of the message off his mind.

During these later years, after hearing of pocket-sized paperbacks, Murray immediately began to write books to be published in that fashion. He thought it was a splendid way to have the teachings of the Christian life at your fingertips, where they could be carried around and read at any time of the day.

Murray's writings still move the emotions, search the conscience, and reveal the sins and shortcomings of many of us with a love and hope born out of an intimate knowledge of the mercy and faithfulness of God.

Countless people have hailed Andrew Murray as their spiritual father and given credit for much of their Christian growth to the influence of his devotional books.